The soldier is the Army. No army is better than its soldiers. The soldier is also a citizen. In fact, the highest obligation and privilege of citizenship is that of bearing arms for one's country.

-George Patton

Acknowledgements and a Note on Military History

As the intention of this book was never to be a strict military history, I have deliberately avoided many organizational and tactical details that could easily have made their appearance. However, the inclusion of information about military hierarchy and logistics is something that I find immensely satisfying, if performed in reasonable quantities. Consequently, to flesh out the historical narrative and ground myself in military credibility, I have been careful to note the contributions of units and commanders both inside and outside Third Army as they pertain to a better understanding of overall events.

With this in mind, I am indebted to the excellent historical narratives of Rick Atkinson and Stephen Ambrose, whose work I have relied upon heavily in constructing what is hopefully an accurate, engaging, and digestible account of the European campaigns. I am also indebted to an author by the name of Norma Rogers, who produced what is probably the only other work available on the 411th. Her records helped to fill in many gaping holes in the sources I had available.

Finally, on a personal level, I am indebted to my parents, Ron and Carla. Through my dad, the magic of history was first made known. Through my mom, I grew to love my grandfather and his legacy. This book would not exist without them.

Andrew Pfeifer, 2/15/16

Introduction

Like millions of Americans, I can count at least one member of the earlier generations of my family who partook in the Second World War as part of the United States Armed Forces. My grandfather, Carl Francis Murray, known affectionately as 'Pappy,' served in a motor support capacity for an anti-aircraft unit that witnessed many of the most awful sights that occurred on the Western European front.

Attached to George Patton's Third Army, his battalion, the 411th AAA, followed the course of the Allied offensive from the beaches of Omaha to the forests of the Ardennes, to the banks of the Rhine, and to the alpine peaks of Berchtesgaden. During the course of the Allied advance across France and Germany from June of 1944 through May of 1945, my grandfather had a front-row seat to some of the most momentous events of the twentieth century.

Of these events, he spoke very little. There were no stories told of specific actions in battle of the type that might adorn the highlights of a unit's history, no remembrances reminiscent of military cinema. He never spoke of D-Day, beyond the fact that he considered himself fortunate to be among those *not* partaking in the initial landing at Omaha Beach. He never boasted of the "confirmed kills" that unit reports would claim whenever flak would down a Luftwaffe flier. We never heard tales of trophies seized from captured Wehrmacht soldiers.

There were a smattering of personal anecdotes, run-ins with famous individuals or places, but rarely ones that involved battle or carnage. Perhaps this was because he himself was never a combat infantryman, or a tanker, or an artillerist, involved in the thickest part of the fighting. Nevertheless, to have spoken to my grandfather was to know that something was being withheld, that the full story was buried somewhere quite deep.

This is obviously something not uncommon among veterans. To say nothing of PTSD, or of its ancestors Battle Fatigue and Shell-Shock, the horrors of war are sufficiently terrible to preclude their discussion in everyday civilian life. But even if it is not possible to delve directly into the psyche of these veterans, it is possible to ask profound questions about how they were able to exist in the line of battle. For my grandfather, what was it that changed him from a civilian in a factory to a soldier in a foxhole. What 'flipped the switch,' so to speak? Did the term 'citizen-soldier' imply that he had achieved a balance between the peaceful and the wartime parts of himself? And, perhaps most poignantly, for those like him that did return, physically and psychologically, how did they go back to The Way Things Were?

The first of these questions has been notably asked by the military scholar Rick Atkinson in his examination of the American army of the early North African campaign. A year prior to the 1942 invasion of Vichy French-held Morocco, the American military was in pitiful shape. 'Flabby,' 'pacifistic, 'yellow,' 'cynical,' and 'discouraged' were adjectives that were thrown around to describe the men of the Arsenal of Democracy. As Atkinson put it, "no hate yet lodged in the bones of American troops, no urge to close with an enemy..."[1]

Yet, the development of hatred was not long delayed. By the time the North African campaign had run its course, the famous war correspondent Ernie Pyle was able to soberly note:

> They [the American soldiers] had made the psychological transition from their normal belief that taking human life was sinful, over to a new professional outlook where killing was a craft. No longer was there anything morally wrong about killing. In fact, it was an admirable thing.
> [They] wanted to see the Germans overrun, mangled, butchered... [they] spoke excitedly of seeing great heaps of dead...[2]

Though Pyle was speaking of the veterans of North Africa, whose number did not include my grandfather, it certainly does not require a difficult leap to apply his observations to units in the other theaters of the war. In expanding this thinking, however, we run into the highly unpalatable notion that the American forces under arms, the lifeblood of the Greatest Generation, may lose their heroic status as citizen-soldiers and that they may be miscast as mere warriors in the strictest sense.

The distinction between between soldiers and warriors has been explored by another military scholar, Max Boot. Per Boot, unlike the soldier, the warrior possesses neither cohesion nor discipline. He is a relic of a bygone era that is preoccupied with a personal role in battle rather than in maintaining a professional formation or achieving a greater objective. Unalloyed hatred also would fall under his purview. [3]

Certainly, in any efficiently-functioning army there is an absolute need for bloodthirstiness and the dehumanization of the enemy. As Boot himself attests, "even modern soldiers try to cultivate warrior virtues." But, in an army made up of men who came from, and intend to return to, the ranks of farmers, factory workers, and clerks, there simply must be some way for their warrior-esque hatred and bile to be left by the wayside. Otherwise, the collective youth of America during WWII should have been unable to abide the return of peace and the advent of the modern world in 1945. [4]

On a personal level, this dichotomy between the ideal citizen-soldier and the hate-filled warrior of Pyle's description is a paramountly uneasy one. Having known my grandfather to be a kindhearted, family-oriented Christian, as far-removed from the world of the battlefield as can be imagined, it is obviously difficult to imagine his thoughts turning to curses against the Hun while under fire. I can speculate that many civilians whose family members served in a combat capacity would feel the same way about their loved ones.

Yet, for all the philosophical hand-wringing that such a notion might engender, it remained largely a moot point for many years. Having only rarely spoken of his time during the war while he was alive, the silence surrounding his experiences became absolute when my grandfather passed away in 2007. Any further inquiry into what might have happened during that time, into what he might have been thinking, seemed consigned to oblivion.

This remained the case until the spring of 2015 when, quite by chance, my family rediscovered a series of boxes of my grandfather's war memorabilia. After having been sorted and stowed away, they were forgotten for a half-decade. Inside them were a historical treasure trove: enlistment papers and orders from the national archives, a smattering of decaying, paper-thin correspondence, daily and after-action reports for the 411th, and, most impactfully, stacks of black-and-white photographs.

The photographs dealt with the entire spectrum of possible wartime experiences. There are shots of him in the early stages of training camp at Camp Davis, North Carolina, in 1942, with notes scrawled on the back complaining that the image fails to do his figure justice. There are shots of him proudly posing next to wrecked Nazi aircraft and goofing up with his buddies. And then there are the glimpses of raw history, pictures of places like the Eagle's Nest or a French crossroads populated by the Third Army.

Perhaps it is the poetic fact that my grandfather's occupation for forty years after the war's end was that of a photographer, but the pictorial form of preservation is an oddly powerful one. To be able to *look* directly at the face of one individual, let alone one family member, as they make their way from waypoint to waypoint through the course of history is something very moving. It transcends the mere parsing of words on paper or in audio transcriptions. Those are powerful and essential, as well, but to *see* a person- that is the essence of understanding a man.

The more that I studied my grandfather's photographs, painstakingly digitizing them, putting them in order of campaign date, connecting them link by link, it became clear that these images could stand for more than just his story. His brothers-in-arms litter the images, soldiers whose names I will never know. They can lay claim to being at the same spots, fighting in the same actions, seeing the same horrors that my grandfather did. Perhaps the most powerful thought that underlies the whole collection is that their stories can also be told through his. Citizen-soldiers all, they can be represented by the wealth of this pictorial evidence and the tale that it reinforces.

In constructing this narrative, I make no claim to rival the military writing of a Stephen Ambrose or Cornelius Ryan. As the Roman historian Livy soberly noted of his own history, "countless others have written on this theme and it may be that I shall pass unnoticed amongst them." Nevertheless, it is my belief that such a profound emotional artifact as my grandfather's photo collection can help to peer in a unique way into the thoughts of a member of the Greatest Generation.

I aim to follow my grandfather through the war in the stories told by these pictures, by the limited accounts that he shared, and by the other scraps of evidence that were recovered in those forgotten boxes. I intend to seek out the nature of his existence in the murky middle-ground of citizen-soldier, between humanity and violence, and to piece this human tale as completely as possible into the larger historical framework of a vast military endeavor. And I make it my goal to use his tale to understand the millions like him - ordinary Americans, pressed into uncommon circumstances. Not killers, but men compelled by necessity to kill.

With all this said, permitting Livy to speak for me again, "I shall find satisfaction in contributing - not, I hope, ignobly - to the labour of putting on record the story of the greatest nation in the world." [5]

June-July

There is something profoundly stirring about a pre-battle speech given by a commander who believes in the righteousness of his cause. Dwight Eisenhower, Supreme Commander of the Allied Expeditionary Force in Europe, certainly qualified as such on the morning of June 6, 1944. As the Allies roused themselves for what would go down in history as *the* Designated Day, Eisenhower's order-of-the-day rang out:

> Soldiers, Sailors and Airmen of the Allied Expeditionary Forces! You are about to embark upon the Great Crusade, toward which we have striven these many months. The eyes of the world are upon you. The hopes and prayers of liberty-loving people everywhere march with you. In company with our brave Allies and brothers-in-arms on other Fronts you will bring about the destruction of the German war machine, the elimination of Nazi tyranny over oppressed peoples of Europe, and security for ourselves in a free world. [1]

"Ike" had reason to wax poetic over the grand invasion force that was about to hit the beaches of Normandy and open up a new Western Front against Nazi Germany. In spite of seemingly interminable delays due to weather, in spite of dissension among the Allied leaders about the location of the attack, some 130,000 soldiers and many thousands of vehicles were being ferried across the English Channel by one of the greatest naval armadas ever assembled. [2]

Under the guns of some 1,200 warships that provided a deafening shore bombardment, the first infantry in the amphibious assault awaited their orders to more ashore [3]. For the Americans, these men were to arrive at the beaches codenamed "Utah", on the eastern neck of the Cotentin peninsula, and "Omaha", about 10 miles further east. British and Canadian troops were to come ashore at the still-more easterly beaches of "Gold," "Juno," and "Sword."

Early that morning, however, prior to any of the amphibious landings, before dawn, came the paratroopers. Specially trained for combat jumps into the enemy's rear, the American 82nd and 101st, and the British 6th, Airborne hit the ground after boarding their C-47 transports late in the night on June 5. Their objective was to disrupt rear-area infrastructure and to keep German reinforcements from reaching the beaches for as long as possible.

The 82nd Airborne had the prime objective of Ste.-Mère-Église, a small town a few miles southwest of Utah Beach. Along with the town of Carentan to the southeast, Ste.-Mère-Église commanded an important road network that linked the port of Cherbourg to the rest of France. The network would have to be held before a breakout offensive, towards Cherbourg or otherwise, could take place. [4]

The division accomplished this objective rapidly - it was a quick, sharp affair, settled by five o'clock on the morning of June 6. A total of ten Germans were killed after house-to-house fighting, and a runner communicated the news of the town's capture to the commander of the 82nd, Major General Matthew Ridgway. Ridgway moved to set up his command post just to the northwest, and the paratroopers dug in for the inevitable German counterattack.

In spite of the quickness with which the town was gained, the division was not neatly concentrated in one piece. On the contrary, the drop had been a confused affair, with regiments of the 101st and 82nd scattered far from their planned arrival points.

By the morning of June 7, however, much had been sorted out. The 2nd and 3rd Battalions of the 505th Parachute Infantry Regiment (PIR) bracketed the northern and southern approaches to the town. To the west lay the important Merderet River which boasted two crossings in the area. Elements of the 507th PIR guarded the southern of these fords, while parts of the 508th, along with Brigadier General James Gavin and the 1st Battalion of the 505th, held the northern crossing.

This triangle, with the town and each of the fords representing one apex apiece, was the ground that needed to be held to protect Utah Beach to the east. Its defenders were behind German lines, without heavy artillery or armored support, close-air cover, or communication with the main

Allied invasion force. They possessed the armaments of light infantry, with the occasional piece of light artillery. And, they had to fend off determined Wehrmacht counterattacks without knowing whether they were to ever be relieved. Gavin recalled,

> Shortly after daylight General Ridgway joined me where the Ste.-Mère-Église road crossed the railroad. Already troopers were speculating that the amphibious landing had not taken place. We had been fighting for a full day and a night [making this June 7], and so far, as near as we knew, we were on our own. General Ridgway and I talked it over and decided that if the amphibious landing for some reason had been called off, we would continue to fight on our present objectives. [5]

The Airborne divisions were ready to hold out on their crucial pieces of land until help came from the sea. That help was coming, and it had hit the beach a handful of hours after the paratroopers themselves had first made landfall.

****

The first unit to arrive on the Normandy beaches was the American 4th Infantry division at Utah. Because of tidal conditions, the vast invasion force (named the 21st Army Group and commanded by the grandiloquent, beret-wearing

Englishman Bernard Montgomery) was forced to stagger its landings from the west to the east. Consequently, the American First Army under Omar Bradley would get first crack at splitting the German defenses at Utah and Omaha Beaches. [6]

At 6:30 AM, after enduring a queasy monotony of waiting aboard troop ships, fighting both seasickness and trepidation about the coming battle, the soldiers of the 4th division made landfall. As the metal ramps of their landing craft splashed into the waist-deep water, the first non-parachutist component of the Great Crusade made contact with Hitler's Atlantic Wall. Joined by the geriatric and cantankerous Brigadier General Theodore Roosevelt, Jr., son of his eponym, the first six hundred assault infantry clambered ashore to clear the way for the subsequent waves.

Problems were encountered immediately. Guide boats for the landing craft were eliminated due to mechanical issues or mine damage. The assault flotilla was unable to distinguish important landmarks across the heavily-bombarded beaches, and the initial force was put ashore more than a mile off-target. LCT's ("Landing Crafts, Tank") that were supposed to ferry armored support in the form of light Sherman tanks to the shore collided and delayed the delivery of the vehicles.

But the saving grace was that little practical resistance was encountered, and the men of the 4th Infantry were able to fan out and clear the beach in record time. After less than two hours of holding the beachhead, boats in subsequent waves were able to land without fear of the formidable shoreline obstacles designed to puncture the metal hulls of any craft that came too close.

Soon enough, the 4th linked up with the paratroopers of the 101st Airborne, and by ten o'clock, the Utah Beach landings could be declared entirely successful. [7]

To the east, however, on Omaha Beach, the story was entirely different. When troops from the 1st and 29th divisions (colorfully named "The Big Red One" and "The Blue and Gray") hit the beach at about the same time as did their counterparts on Utah, they encountered much fiercer resistance than at the latter.

On Omaha, pillboxes and machine gun nests were strewn densely over the land that overlooked the beaches, with carefully-sited artillery ensuring that there was nowhere on the sand that was untouchable by Nazi guns. Further, the German defenders had been reinforced by additional troops in the preceding months. The initial companies ashore across the width of the beach took horrendous losses, many men falling dead from machine gun bullets the instant the ramps of their landing craft dropped.

Progress was slow, costly, and supremely bloody. It was only by the latter part of the morning that inroads were finally made into the German lines on the western half of the beach, and elements of the Big Red One were able to knife inland, away from the coast.

By the end of D-Day, as planners prepared to turn their invasion calendars to D+1, a total of 12,000 casualties had been taken by the Allies. In exchange, a narrow beachhead had been won that in places was little deeper than a mile. Though the airborne forces still remained scattered, with the 82nd stranded at Ste.-Mère-Église, and though huge numbers of men and materièl still needed transported across the English Channel, a toehold had been established. It was a shallow one, indeed, but Germany could not ignore the fact that a Western Front had been opened.

****

In the immediate aftermath of D-Day, the American forces on continental soil could field the initial elements of two Corps. The VII, under "Lightning" Joe Collins, was lodged at Utah. Its 4th Division would soon be joined by the 9th and 90th. They would be brought up to fan out into the ancient French countryside, assist the airborne troops, and seize Cherbourg and the Cotentin. The disposition at Omaha was similar, with the V Corps under General Leonard Gerow encompassing the Big Red One and the 29th Divisions. They would soon be reinforced by the 2nd.

Assault infantry aside, both Corps contained an impressive menagerie of support troops that were necessary to propel a modern army in a successful campaign. Among these, the VII Corps could boast a sizable detachment of engineers, including the 1st Engineer Special Brigade and the 1106th Engineer Combat Group. These units would serve the role as combat engineers, advancing under fire, side-by-side with the infantry, removing the huge steel obstacles and mines that German forces had seeded densely on the beaches. They would also act in a logistical role, supervising the disembarkation of supplies and men from the endless tide of landing craft that floated ashore, building airstrips, and turning beaches into ports to sustain the immense sea of humanity spilling onto French soil.

    For obtaining the heavier firepower necessary to dominate a modern battlefield, old-fashioned "boots-on-the-ground" were not quite sufficient. To supplement the masses of standard issue, semi-automatic, M1 Garand rifles that an infantry division provided, massed armor, artillery, and aerial superiority was necessary. Shortly into the campaign, the Allies could boast an immense numerical superiority in all these areas. At the beginning of it, though, only dominance in the air was available. Mobile heavy weapons were limited to the Shermans that did not end up at the bottom of the ocean and to what vehicles were succesfully unloaded off of their LST's.

    However, when viewed in isolation, the depth of the Allies' air superiority in the West is sufficiently staggering to make any other deficiencies seem trifling. Apart from the sizable and experienced RAF forces that had defended England so resolutely in the days of the Blitz and had committed to thousand-bomber-strong nighttime raids against German targets, the famous American Eighth Force under Jimmy Doolittle added its 1,635 planes to the aerial swarms available to the invasion. Between these masses of B-17, B-24, and B-26 bombers, the Army Air Forces had the firepower necessary to maintain close-air-support for the largest possible front and to pulverize rear-area German logistics to the point that airstrips and railroads were barely usable. [8]

A similar edge was owned by Allied fighters, with the reliable P-47 Thunderbolt and the newcomer P-51 Mustang significantly thinning the ranks of available Luftwaffe pilots and planes in the months leading up to the invasion. Thanks in no small part to this damage, the Luftwaffe in the vicinity of Normandy could scrape together aircraft numbering a few hundred to match against the Allies' armadas numbering in the thousands. German soldiers would quip that "American planes were gray, British planes black, and Luftwaffe planes invisible." [9]

In spite of this aerial domination, ground forces still needed to be able to fight for themselves in the event of a Luftwaffe raid happening when nearby air cover was unavailable, as even the Allied air forces could not be everywhere at once. It was to this end that mobile anti-aircraft artillery (AA or AAA) was attached to infantry and armor formations throughout the duration of the Western Front. These AAA units were independent groups that could be separated from larger ground commands and redeployed as needed.

American AAA forces boasted a combination of three primary weapons. 50-caliber Browning machine guns made up the low-end of the firepower spectrum, providing an incredible firing rate of some 500 rounds per minute. Apart from their destructive ability against airborne targets, crews found the lethal rapidity of their barrels to be exceptionally useful against enemy ground personnel and light vehicles. A step up on the firepower scale presents the 40mm cannon, which could hurl armor-piercing, 1.96-lb. shells at a rate of 120 per minute at approaching aircraft. These guns were famous for managing to destroy a number of German V1 rockets mid-flight. Finally, the heavy 90mm gun was used to destroy planes flying at higher altitudes. Also serving as an anti-tank weapon, both it and the 40mm represented upgrades the US Army had made earlier in its WWII-era expansion. By some, including my grandfather, the bigger guns would be nicknamed 'ack-ack' guns, for their 'AA' designation.

Anti-air formations were organized at the battalion level, with each battalion possessing four Fire batteries and one Headquarters battery. Battalions were given the designation of either "Gun" battalions or "Automatic Weapons" battalions. Battalions who received the latter designation towed 40mm weapons into battle, while those with the former manned the larger 90mm pieces.

For the VII Corps, its anti-aircraft protection consisted of the independent 11th AAA Group, attached for the duration of the initial Normandy campaign. The guns of the 11th covered all the possible roles of anti-aircraft protection, including those of semi-specialized anti-tank artillery. They were divided into an arithmetical slew of units: the 81st, 116th, 535th, 474th, and 552nd were among those represented. Also part of this command was the 411th, a "Gun" battalion typical in almost every way. Except, for me, it was my grandfather's.

****

The 411th had begun its existence two years before under the purview of the coastal artillery, who possessed the rather-obsolete mission of protecting American shores via the usage of large cannon. First constituted on May 21, 1942, and officially activated several months later, the 411th, like many AAA outfits, was a byproduct of the army leadership scrambling to equip themselves against a then-superior Luftwaffe.

As part of this anti-aircraft mobilization, the coastal artillery, who still officially claimed ownership of AAA units, constructed multiple training camps across the country. The geographical diversity of these sites is striking. Savannah, Riverside, Houston, and Cape Cod all could claim a nearby base that trained the boys who would kill Luftwaffe fliers. Wilmington, North Carolina, also boasted such a site: Camp

Davis, near the still-extant Marine base at Camp LeJeune. Some recruits wound up moving from one army training site to another, remembering more or less about one location depending on their particular experiences there. My grandfather found himself routed through Camp Davis after training at Fort Eustis in Virginia, and it is there that our family's memories of him in World War II begin.

Photographs of Camp Davis show the type of starkly-built army town that could just as well have been located in New Mexico or California as in North Carolina, and perhaps that was part of the point. Wooden barracks, wide-open roads lined with solitary telephone poles, and various training ranges for the 40mm and 90mm cannon marked the most obvious landmarks on the base. The camp was considered to be comparatively homey, relative to other army facilities such as Fort Eustis, and by military standards it certainly could have been declared a comfortable abode. At the very least, the army tried to keep the men busy in their off-duty hours with various sports and social activities. But, in spite of the numerous recreational opportunities that were provided (among other things, the base's football team was sufficiently powerful to beat some college squads), the purpose of the base was anything but recreational. [10]

Images of my grandfather from this time show him with that distinctively American jaunt, the same reserved, sublime goofiness that is evident in so many pictures of GI's. A tall (over six feet) and well-built (189-pound) man even by modern standards, the cocked head and Mona Lisa smile add to the mischievous aura that, in various forms across the army, would come to manifest itself a continent away with scrawlings of "Kilroy Was Here" across hundreds of Axis structures.

As a civilian, and as my grandfather's grandson, these images are profound: they show a man whose existence is undergoing transformation into a military realm. They speak to a shift in nature greater than most will ever experience in their lives, from the peaceful clamor of a semi-skilled industrial foreman to the battlefield, where death is a possibility at a moment's notice. In these images of and before his time at Camp Davis are encapsulated the middle stage of a metamorphosis, somewhere between full-time civilian and temporary, but fully-occupied, citizen-soldier. As if to emphasize that the transformation was not a process that could be easily completed, the following was scrawled, in my grandfather's italicized handwriting, on the back of one of the photographs:

> They were trying to make [me] smile. I know that I am not that fat.

The cares of a civilian life, of appearance over function, are something that do not, and, perhaps, should not, go easily away.

After training throughout 1942 and 1943 at the various AAA facilities spread across the east coast, the 411th and its sister battalions traveled across the turbulent Atlantic during the winter of 1943-44. The unit made its home amid the English countryside for the next five months, training, enjoying the camaraderie of the local Britons, and, above all, waiting for D-Day.

My grandfather never kept much track of the journey across the ocean or of his time in the UK. There were never any stories of wild encounters in Scottish pubs or impromptu football matches with enthusiastic Welshmen. He had reached the rank of Staff Sergeant by this point, overseeing a contingent of Battery D's motor pool. Although the crazy days of massed Luftwaffe sorties over British skies were long gone by this point in the war, the guns of the 411th were still pointed skyward to guard the infrastructure that would support the coming invasion. His role, then, was ensuring the mobility

Posing next to a destroyed Me-109. This particular craft was destroyed while still on the ground. Note the presence of the battery's mascot.

*'They were trying to make me smile.
I know I am not that fat.'*

and supply of the 90mm cannon, wherever in the rolling hills of the shires they redeployed.

As May of 1944 gave way to June, the 411th and the rest of the 11th AAA group made their way south towards the embarkation points for the invasion. There, they encountered the rest of the vast Allied legions that were about to set off for France and made their final preparations for crossing the Channel with the larger body of VII Corps. [11]

The first elements of the 411th made landfall on continental soil on D+3, June 9. At 8 AM, Battery A began to disembark on Utah Beach, the western end of the Allied salient where the entirety of the 11th was to provide its support. It took two days for the battery to make it ashore, but the landing itself was orderly and without incident.

The same could not be said for the other pieces of the battalion. C Battery did not land until June 11. When it did, it found itself on Omaha Beach. It defended the landings there until it finally made the trek over to Utah three days later. Batteries B and D found themselves split in two, their strength divided between Utah and Omaha. The latter of these contingents included my grandfather. This group had to make an anabasis similar to that of Battery C before linking back up on June 14. The 411th thus experienced the same fog of war that Teddy Roosevelt, Jr., had encountered at the beginning of the invasion. The Normandy landings were at least consistent in their confusion.

With the battalion's strength finally concentrated in a single area, its mission of providing a screen against Nazi airpower could begin in earnest. All of the batteries engaged their fair share of fliers, with the after-action-report (AAR) for Battery D claiming the engagement of twenty-four enemy aircraft (EA).

Anti-aircraft AAR's are a peculiar document. They read as a mixture of a quarterback's passing statistics and the boastful diary of an Old West gunslinger, talking up the number of men slain in a gunfight. For the month of June, Battery C was two-for-nineteen: "...the battery engaged nineteen EA. Claims for destruction of two enemy planes during the period are pending."

    C battery had made those two kills near Ste.-Mère-Église, where Gavin's parachutists had dug in back on D-Day proper. Since then, the front had inched south and west, and my grandfather and his comrades most likely never encountered the airborne troops. Regardless, at the rate they were advancing, the Allies would start to reach *bocage* country, a vast region of northern France that consisted of ancient, interlocking hedgerows, within a few days. Stupendously thick and requiring unreasonable amounts of explosives to clear, the hedgerows created hellish conditions for the infantry that waded through them. German snipers and mortars made the darkened alleys between the rows a true killing ground for the VII Corps, and Allied forward movement ground to a halt in the face of the unforeseen flora. [12]

    The 411th was fortunate enough to not become ensconced in this unforgiving terrain. It was still entrenched back in the original landing area keeping watch over the local transportation hubs that would supply incursions deeper into France. D Battery itself was dug in near the small town of Carentan, which had been the site of heavy fighting involving the 101st during the initial landings. There, it recorded its only confirmed kill during the initial months on the Western Front.

    This achievement is reflected nowhere except in a

pair of brief notes in army AAR's. I can only speculate what my grandfather's reaction would have been. Elation on concretely contributing to the war effort, pensiveness on taking a part in the destruction of another human life, and apathy after seeing enough non-combat time in the army to simply want to return home are all possible. Yet, the images that have survived of him standing next to destroyed Nazi craft like a hunter next to a kill do not paint the picture of a reluctant warrior. The wrecked planes, emblazoned with Iron Crosses, are flanked by a soldier who is smiling, proud to be present at, and involved in, the *Ragnarok*, the dismembering of the Reich.

****

      Whatever my grandfather's personal thoughts may have been over his men's guns finally slaying an enemy, Battery D and the 411th did not move forward with the main body of Bradley's forces. As June turned to July, and as the quagmire in the Normandy bocage became increasingly unacceptable, First Army and its aircover was tasked with breaking the stalemate against the Wehrmacht in a major offensive to the south, codenamed *Operation Cobra*.

      The goal of the attack was to get American columns into the French heartland and away from the cramped lodgings of Omaha and Utah Beaches. Once given some breathing room, the enormous tide of armor and men that was cascading into the Channel ports could maneuver freely and envelop and destroy the German forces. This was a doctrine of offensive maneuver and firepower concentration writ large. With open country, the numerical advantage held by American armored forces could be fully exploited.

Cobra's front centered on Collins's VII Corps, now divorced from the 11th AAA Group. This front was tasked with waiting for American airpower to blast a rectangular hole in the German lines along the road between the villages of St. Lô and Pérriers, a northwest-to-southeast axis. The VII Corps would then spearhead some 15 divisions on a drive through this killzone, breaking through German road and rail lines and swinging further south through France. These fifteen divisions included a number of stalwarts from the initial actions in Normandy, including the Big Red One. [13]

The peculiar danger of this offensive lay in the nature of the aerial killzone desired by Bradley. Namely, it embodied "danger close" bombing, in that some 1,200 yards would separate the front-most assault troops from the first bombs. Given how inaccurate "precision" bombing was throughout the war, this was hardly an adequate margin of distance to avoid friendly fire. If nothing else, the decision to provide bombing cover at such a distance underscores the role of the individual in war planning. Per Bradley, "War has neither the time nor heart to concern itself with the individual and the dignity of man."

The *Cobra* offensive was delayed until July 24 due to poor weather conditions. When it finally got underway, P-47's, B-17's, and B-24's pummeled the killzone with thousands of tons of bombs. As could be tragically expected, friendly casualties were heavy. The 30th Division, "Old Hickory," was hit especially hard. Many of the bombers dropped their payloads short by miles, eliciting massed curses among the infantry who survived the unintentional onslaught.

In spite of this inaccuracy, the airstrikes ultimately had the intended effect on the German forces. The Panzer Lehr division, an elite armored formation, was in the line facing the VII Corps. By the end of the bombardment, it's commander was forced to dejectedly report that his men were "half-crazed" and "running in circles." [14]
Confusion had been achieved, and Collins was able to launch the exploitation phase of the offensive on the 26th.

Along with the 30th Division, a handful of infantry and armored units surged through the breach, rapidly seizing hedgerow country that would previously have required days to overtake. Nazi resistance crumbled, and a vast green tide of men and Shermans poured south to cut off the remaining formations in what was becoming a sizable and vulnerable pocket. The German army, which earlier in the war had been the master of envelopment and close-air-support in defeating French and Russian forces, had been bested in its own doctrine.

By the first dawn of August, the US Army in France

was on the move. The 411th was still stuck in the northern extremities of the Allied beachhead, but that would soon change.

Bradley received a promotion to head the 12th Army Group, complementing Monty's 21st Army Group to the east. The 12th would encompass both Bradley's old First Army and a new force: the Third Army.

The catalyst that prompted this reshuffling? None other than the arrival of 'Old Blood 'n Guts,' George Patton.

****

Five decades down the road, the storming and subsequent defense of the Normandy beaches has long been entrenched in the history books and has entered into the realm of fictionalized entertainment. Steven Spielberg's *Saving Private Ryan* falls in the latter category and is rightly regarded as one of the greatest war movies of all time. From its first release in July of 1998, it was hailed for its gripping depiction of WWII infantry combat. The opening sequence depicting the bloodbath of the initial landing at Omaha Beach is particularly renowned.

My grandfather had always been a devoted fan of media that chronicled war and combat. The first introduction that I received to the classic *Patton* had been via the old VHS tape that he kept in the bowels of their wooden TV stand. John Wayne's gunfighter-westerns would always hold his attention, especially when marathons of them were rerun on cable. And, when I was old enough to play video games, I taught him enough about the concept for him to experience one of the entries in the *Medal of Honor* series. He happily passed that day's afternoon shooting up virtual Axis formations.

But as much as he loved the visceral experiences that these images could offer, the message that he would send about them, first to my mom, later to me, were always the same: the movies, the shows, the games, were, unsurprisingly, completely unlike real combat. I would suspect that most every veteran would agree.

When *Saving Private Ryan* was released fifty-odd years to the month after his time spent entrenched outside of Utah, however, my grandfather's excitement about the film was elevated to a level beyond merely that of viewing a pleasurable-but-inaccurate war picture. Perhaps here would be the movie that could capture the agony of war and encapsulate his travails such that others, noncombatants, could understand.

If the civilian reviews and the hype surrounding the picture were any indication, it certainly could. Roger Ebert, that guru of all things film, hailed it for "say[ing] things about war that are as complex and difficult as any essayist could possibly express, and [doing] it with broad, strong images, with violence, with profanity, with action, with camaraderie."

For Ebert, it was "as graphic as any war footage I've ever seen." [15]

But perhaps that was the point. The movie, or any war movie, for that matter, could never be anything more real, more engaging, than war *footage*.

The audience does not have to worry about an actual 88mm shell destroying their lounge chairs. There is no likelihood of their having to perform a battlefield tracheotomy, or of having to dig a foxhole in the ground as quickly as they possibly can. There is definitely no physical reason for them to jump at the sounds of the simulated gunfire.

Something that I suspect is stupendously obvious for all veterans bears repeating for us civilians: there is no way to reenact real combat, on the silver screen or otherwise.

Suffice it to say that my grandfather walked away from the movie disappointed. Years later, my mom would recount to me his final judgment on Spielberg's work: it was close, a good movie, but *not quite it*.

Yet, his dismissal of the veracity of war movies never seemed to diminish the force impacted upon him by other parts of daily life that evoked memories of his time in Europe. A prime example of this was his reaction to the sounds of fireworks on the Fourth of July or New Year's. These would render him profoundly miserable and uneasy, a response to being exposed to incessant hours of gunfire. I suppose it could be said, then, that the worst stimuli, the type of ghastly revelations and recollections that can shake a man, are the types that cannot be communicated in a format understandable to others. As Tim O'Brien put it, about a different war, in a different time:

> Often in a true war story there is not even a point, or else the point doesn't hit you until twenty years later, in your sleep, and you wake up and shake your wife and start telling the story to her, except when you get to the end you've forgotten the point again . [16]

The exact 'point' for my grandfather as he was shuddering at those fireworks or shaking his head with mild disappointment at Spielberg's masterpiece was something he may have found prior to his death. But, if he did, by its very nature, it would have stayed with him, and him alone.

August

On August 1, as the first step in getting an increasing number of Allied forces onto the continent, the paper strength of Bradley's command effectively doubled. Succeeded by Courtney Hodges, the leader of the First Army ascended to the command of the 12th Army Group. The development that prompted these shifts in the American order-of-battle was the activation of the Third Army under General George Patton.

Patton is a man who tends to elicit superlatives from those who attempt to describe him. This is perhaps exactly what would be expected of someone whose professional resume included hunting Pancho Villa's henchmen, using Army cavalry for crowd-control in Washington, D.C., and, alongside Eisenhower, pioneering armored maneuvers. He had an innate feel for the modern war of maneuver that characterized the actions of his armored columns, and his views on overall strategy were quite simple: commanders should launch "violent attacks everywhere with everything." [9] He was aggressive, profane, and hot-headed in his dealings with his fellow officers and superiors. At various times, Bradley, Eisenhower, and especially Montgomery were recipients of his scathing disapproval.

During the months prior to August, 1944, Patton was kept in England leading a phantom army with the fake objective of enacting a second coastal landing. The deception was successful enough that a substantial number of German forces were kept immobile, waiting for the thrust from Patton that would never come. As he was perceived by the Nazi high-command to be the Allies' best general, it seemed inconceivable that he would be kept on the sidelines of the war's most audacious thrust.

Patton's absence from center stage was a direct consequence of his big mouth in dealing with the media and of his slapping of a battle-fatigued soldier during the Sicilian campaign (for Patton, PTSD was no better than cowardice). Nevertheless, he was reluctantly forgiven and found his way back into the line to command the newly-minted Third Army. [1]

Liberating a French town.
The girl in the foreground is most likely Annette.

The AAR's of the 411th reflect Patton's ascension to leadership almost immediately. Newly attached to the anti-aircraft contingent assigned to protect the Third Army, the battalion's reported locations for the month of August change every few days. Following a corridor opened by the 4th Armored Division, the 411th moved past the western edge of the wasteland created by *Cobra* and through the French towns of Coutances and Avranches, reaching the latter on August 6. Five days earlier, the 4th Armored had already reached Rennes, the capital of Brittany. In both cases, and in most cases every time the Allies reached a French city, the Gallic citizenry were exuberant to meet their liberators.

    Years later, my grandfather told a story of meeting a young French girl in the ruins of one of the towns liberated by the Third Army. The child, on seeing the American soldiers, found a solitary egg, an object of great value in the devastated countryside. She timidly marched up to my grandfather and handed the egg to him, a meek offering of thanksgiving. She gave her name as Annette, although my grandfather's atrocious grasp of French would have prevented much further conversation. Her parents were never mentioned; they may very well have been killed by the tremendous shelling and bombing that preceded the Allies' advance.

    If nothing else, Patton's troops were appreciated for what they were doing, even by children who had seen their young lives torn asunder.

****

As the Third Army barreled deeper into France, Bradley and Patton made the decision to split the forces of the new formation into western and eastern contingents. The former included the Third Army's spearhead, the 4th Armored, and would advance towards the port of Brest on the Atlantic. It would eventually find itself bogged down in frustratingly unproductive sieges, slowly taking ports that would never actually be used.

The rest of Patton's forces, consisting of XV and XX Corps, pivoted east, with the city of Rennes as their axis. Galloping in the general direction of Paris, the Third Army reached a tactical crossroads by mid-August. After pushing through Laval and Le Mans, Patton's men had been ordered to move north towards the towns of Argentan and Falaise.

There, a large number of German troops, some twenty divisions, found themselves defending a semi-elliptical position against Canadian and British troops from the north and Hodges's American First Army in the west. Ike and Bradley believed that Patton's columns could provide the final piece to completely hem in the German formations and bag the entire force, thus closing what would come to be known as the "Falaise Pocket."

To accomplish this, Third Army would need to weaken its main push to the east, towards Paris, and redirect substantial resources to this shorter-distance envelopment. Patton, who always liked to think in broad strokes and massed forces over large distances, was not happy with the change, though he ultimately acquiesced to Bradley's orders and detached General Wade Haislip's XV Corps for the operation. Haislip's lead columns, actually French armored units outfitted with American-made tanks, arrived in Alençon on August 12 and began the trek north that was to link them up with their Canadian counterparts.

During this drive, the 411th underwent its fourth reassignment of the month (evidently the fast-moving Patton rubbed off on the logisticians in charge of battalion assignments). After finding themselves first under the 207th AAA Group, then the 24th, and then the 27th, my grandfather's battery was finally assigned to the 23rd AAA Group on August 14. The 23rd has the role of protecting the XV Corps, which by then had already overrun Argentan and was not far from touching the southeastern point of the German pocket.

Had the status quo remained unchanged, my family history may well have reflected some war story involving Haislip's men attempting to envelop the cut-off Nazi forces. As it were, though, Bradley intervened. On August 15, perhaps to soothe Patton's irritation at losing a whole Corps to what he viewed as a sideshow, or perhaps because of slower-than-expected Canadian progress southward, roughly half of Haislip's troops, including the 411th, were given back to Patton for his eastward drive.

The elements of the XV Corps that were left to assault the Falaise Pocket participated in a thorough smashing of the Nazi forces concentrated therein. Massed aerial assaults and heavy artillery fire destroyed German armor and vehicles by the hundreds, and many German prisoners, sick of the ceaseless hail of high-explosives, surrendered with appropriately-profane calls of "Merde pour la guerre!" [2]

Nevertheless, the damage could have been much worse, and many German troops that could have been captured and eliminated from the war were permitted to escape out of the pocket. One thing they would not be able to do, however, was to mount a thorough defense of Paris and the Seine, the next major landmarks on the route east through France.

The honor of taking the City of Lights would go to Patton's men, although they were not Americans. The same Frenchmen of the XV Corps, Jacques Phillippe LeClerc's 2nd Armored Division, that had initially led the charge against the southern flank of the Falaise Pocket, entered the southwestern corner of Paris on August 25, preceding Charles de Gaulle by a matter of hours. American troops followed shortly behind the French and, after brief mob warfare between Parisians and Nazis reminiscent of a stylized Delacroix scene, the German troops in the city either retired or were captured.

They left behind them a city surprisingly unscathed. De Gaulle commented that the only thing missing from the old rooms of the Ministry of War was the government itself. The Louvre, the Arc de Triomphe, the Eiffel Tower, and the vast majority of the architectural wonders of Paris were unharmed by four years of Nazi occupation. So, too, was the relaxed Parisian way of life: August 25 happened to be the feast day of St. Louis, and, regardless of street fighting, sniper fire, and massed armored columns entering the city, that called for a punctual and celebratory lunch hour. [5,6]

In the coming weeks, various contingents of the Allied forces would make their way through liberated Paris, reveling in the exuberance of the joyful French crowds. Ceremonial marches down the Champs-Élysées were not the norm, however. Like most outfits, the 411th was occupied elsewhere.

****

In the days prior to LeClerc's entering the city, meteorological conditions in central France were dreadful, bad enough to keep American air cover grounded throughout the region. German aircraft, however, were willing to brave the dreary skies. They had little choice but to throw everything possible at the relentless Allied tide.

August 21 was the first day that air supriority was not available, which meant that ground-based anti-aircraft was pushed to the forefront. Although the terrible days of 1939 and 1940, when Stuka dive bombers could smash troop movements outright, had not returned, the much-reduced Luftwaffe, if unchecked, could still serve as a serious impediment for the Allied advance. This was especially true at crossing-points over the Seine river, the ancient carotid artery of Gaul that was forever linked with Paris. A millenium earlier, the river had hosted Viking armies on their way to sack the city. In 1944, Americans were crossing it to save Paris, and, massed as they were at the scattered fords on the river's western bank, they needed protection from threats above to reach the eastern side.

XV Corps's 23rd AAA was more than up to the task of giving this protection. The elements that accompanied the most advanced units deployed at Mantes and Rosny-sur-Seine, two adjoining locales about thirty miles from the outer edge of Paris. The 411th found themselves at the former, Mantes, where the river's course veers sharply right, towards the south, creating a sudden concavity in the terrain.

French country road crossing, as demarcated by a large cross - a prime site for AAA defense.

There, over the course of the 21st and 22nd of August, the anti-aircraft put on a stupendous display of aerial marksmanship that closed any hope the Luftwaffe had of exploiting the temporary dearth of Allied airpower. The 411th participated as fully in this show as any battalion did. Setting up in a lowland surrounded by heights on three sides, A, B, and C Batteries relied on Battery D to lure German fliers into their kill zones. Like the lead dogs in a Victorian hunt, the battery's rapid-fire Browning guns would herd their prey into a constrained area, where the concentrated flak of the remainder of the battalion would promptly finish the job. The army could certainly be proud of the synergy between its antiair weapons. [3,4]

All told, the 23rd AAA downed a confirmed 43 German planes during those two days. This is a staggering total, considering that German aircraft at the start of the Normany campaign numbered only a few hundred. The 411th accounted for 19 of those kills, although only three were attributed directly to D Battery. Acting as an enabler in combat takes it toll on the stat sheet, even in official AAR's.

The superiority of the ground-based batteries was sufficiently impressive to warrant commendations from all sides. Colonel J.B. Fraser, commanding officer of the 23rd, crowed that the entire array of battalions under his command achieved "one of the outstanding achievements of anti-aircraft during the war." General Haislip singled out the 411th in particular, giving the men an official commendation and dubbing it "...a first class fighting unit... playing a large part in the liquidation of the German Army" and lauding their "splendid accomplishment" along the banks of the Seine. Even the normally staid battalion AAR noted the battalion's "participation in the making of AA history." [7,8]

All things considered, the 411th and my grandfather certainly did their duty. There was no march into Paris after the crossings were secure, but they were a step closer to the war's end.

****

The episode on the bank of the Seine is, unfortunately, one of the episodes of my grandfather's history that is most devoid of personal information. I have already mentioned his predilection of not speaking about his wartime remembrances. August of 1944 was one of the worst victims of this practice. If it were not for the unit's records and Norma Rogers's excellent compendium of letters related to the 411th, I would not have known that he had any connection at all with the liberation of Paris. The month of August will join the Battle of the Bulge and the time his unit spent in the Alps late in the war as those occasions which are most painful in their silence.

They are the most painful because of where he was, both in space and in time. He sat right next to, or right in the heart of, events that any historian would deem to be truly great. There must have been nuances of the fighting, relationships with his comrades, wry remarks that could grace the pages of history. As a lover of biographical history, it is anguishing to think about what might have been. The idea of putting a literary, non-fictional Marlborough in character, on the scene of a great engagement, is the dream of many writers.

It is times like this that I force myself to remember that, along with whatever pre-20th century notions of glory could have been preserved from oblivion by hearing of the specifics of his soldierly life, there is an undeoubtedly greater number of memories and stories that would be ghastly, gory, and miserable. When confronted with a void in history, it is a comfort to remember the Tolstoyan proverb that, perhaps, there are fewer things that can be learned in the heat of combat than might be first imagined. I suspect Leo Tolstoy would have been as proud of the American citizen-soldiers as he was of his own Russian peasants. Both were not combatants at heart. They would drive their enemies back ferociously, but, at day's end, they wanted to return to their homes.

****

One thing I learned about my grandfather, though, serene and peaceful man that he was, was that his Army swagger, his combat training, never fully left him. My family and I found this out firsthand during one August evening when we found ourselves at the primary Catholic church in Liberty Boro. Named St. Mark's, after the apostle, it is sited near the southern edge of town, about a ten minute drive from my grandparents' old house.

Viewed from the nearby road, driving northbound, it appears as a triangular prism. The main church boasts a peculiar number of polygonal glass panes on the front, stained with abstract religious scenery. The windows lend an appearance that sharply distinguishes the structure from the neighboring houses. The latter are pleasant abodes, yet their aluminum and brick fronts do not convey the same sense of openness as that given by the glassy veneer across the street.

Immediately adjacent to the church, on the southern side, is a large, green, well-manicured field of grass. On the northern side lies the main church parking lot.

For a few days in every August, like many Catholic churches, St. Mark's hosted a grand parish festival. The parking lot swelled with old-fashioned pinstripe carnival booths that held dozens of amusements and raffles. Prize wheels, target games, and musicians filled the lot to bursting as parishioners and family members came out for a last summer hurrah before the start of the school year.

The fair could also claim a sprawling, musty flea market, replete with old comics and toys, a petting zoo, and an impressive Eastern European food scene. As a child, I eagerly embraced both the cheap Batman comics and the enormous portions of haluski. Suffice it to say that the pilgrimage that my grandparents, my parents, and I would always make to the fair was a highlight of the summer.

For this particular sojourn, the five of us had parked near the far end of the lot, furthest away from the bustle of the fair. We were on our way to get something to eat, walking along the sidewalk by the church. My grandfather led our little column, and I trailed shortly behind him.

On the path in front of us sat a pair of adolescents, perhaps thirteen years old. They were dressed in the clothing typically appropriated by young teenagers who wish to appear tough: baggy pants, oversized t-shirts, baseball caps. Lounging on the walkway, their apathetic expressions did not suggest any awareness of the formation coming their way, or of any inclination to move.

My grandfather had by this time built up a full head of steam and had no intention of stopping for the obstacle in front of him. With his quarter-zip pullover and his slick wooden cane moving in lockstep with him, he cast the appearance of a soldier wading into battle with bayonet fixed.

As he approached the youths, the movement in his cane became more rapid, side-to-side as if he were swatting flies. In a temperate voice that was still filled with authority, he proceeded to order the youths out of our way, all the while brushing their backsides towards the curb with the cane.

Sullenly and slowly they yielded, as if unconsciously recognizing that they were up against a quietly unstoppable force. As they made enough of a passage for our party of five to pass, my grandfather marched forward triumphantly.

This was obviously a small moment, perhaps even a trifling moment. But, for the briefest of instants fifty years after he had left the army, fifty years after his ack-ack guns filled the skies over the Seine to keep the Luftwaffe off Haislip's columns, my grandfather could act as the protector of a column once again. The flak had been exchanged for a cane, the armored formations for his family, but the instinct was still the same.

September-November

The Third Army's race across France continued for a few more weeks after the capture of Paris, Patton urging on his columns like a man possessed. He claimed that, if properly supported, he could breach the German border by early September. At the rate the German army was retreating, or, more accurately, disintegrating, he may have been right – it was reported that some Nazi forces had run out of white flags to use for surrendering and were waving chickens instead. [1]

To the north, Monty's forces and Hodges's First Army had crossed into Belgium and, by mid-September, had taken the imporant port of Antwerp. On the eastern fronts, German fortunes were crumbling in a similar fashion: the Soviets were on the march, and the regime's allies were starting to defect. All told, it certainly appeared that the Wehrmacht could fall apart at any minute, toppling Hitler's state with it.

In the meantime, however, Patton had to watch with furious exasperation as his grand armored offensive ground to a halt. There were a variety of reasons for the stoppage in Third Army's great end-around, but by far the most significant was a simple lack of fuel. In the course of the Allies' race towards the west, supply lines, anchored around the Channel ports, had become critically extended. As American and British forces approached the German border, it was now necessary to move vast amounts of ammunition, food, and gasoline over the entire breadth of France. For all the logistical expertise that the United States Army possessed, this would remain a tall order.

The final result of the months of autumn, 1944, as it pertained to the men of the Third Army was an effective stalemate. This was certainly not the case everywhere, though. To the north, in the Low Countries, Montgomery would receive attention as British troops and the refreshed 82nd and 101st Airborne undertook the bloody engagements of Operation Market Garden. Designed to be a dagger-thrust through a soft-spot of the German lines, it relied on a rapid taking of Dutch towns and the bridges that connected them.

Initial airborne jumps to take these locations and establish preliminary control over them were made on September 17, including jumps by the reconstituted 505th PIR, part of the initial boots-on-the-ground on D-Day. British armored columns were to follow closely behind, but, over the next week of fighting, the timing of the advance fell apart. Recriminations ensued when the tank formations were unable to reach their final objectives. The elite airborne troops, pressed into service as inadequately-supported line infantry, suffered terrible casualties, and the campaign degenerated into miserable, static warfare. The phrase 'A Bridge Too Far,' the title of Cornelius Ryan's history of the campaign, sums up the entirety of the experience. There would be no quick movement into northern Germany. [2]

In contrast to the bloody actions chronicled by Ryan, the AAR's of the 411th for much of September are exceptionally quiet, surely to Patton's chagrin. The phrase "no action" appears frequently, and the most exciting entry is a familiar "out of gas." ³

In this state, the broader Third Army rolled into Nancy, just south of the prized city of Metz, on September 14. Little additional progress east would be made by September 20, when the 411th caught up with Patton's vanguard. Indeed, there would be essentially no progress made for quite some time. Movement towards the east, in the direction of the oxbow-shaped French-German border, was slowed by torrential rains and the ongoing lack of basic supplies. It would be early December before Third Army's lines touched the Rhine in any appreciabe force, let alone spear into the Reich's heartland. Patton would have to wait until later to join Caesar as an intruder into Germania. The 411th waited with him.

During this interim period, the battalion did double duty as both a AAA outfit and a makeshift field artillery battery, taking a cue from German 88mm cannon operators. Apart from this crossover, though, the formal activities of the unit were uneventful. They stayed in much the same place, near Nancy and the close-by Pont-à-Mousson. While there, the battalion blazed away at the diminished Luftwaffe and at enemy infantry petrified by the American preponderance in artillery strength. ⁴

In spite of the static nature of these months, the personal stories from my grandfather that have survived seem to peak at this time. As usual, dating these tales to a precise time involves some guesswork, since he never left any definitive chronological information. But, the jigsaw pieces of oral history fit right into the larger picture of Autumn '44 – the weather, the nearness to Metz, the sense that the war just might be close to a finale, all make this location feel right. So, they shall be placed here.

If nothing else, the *citizen* part of the ciziten-soldier comes out strongly during these months. He, like his comrades, had clearly not forgotten about home. Although it was imperative to concentrate on not getting killed by enemy fire, he and they could let their thoughts drift to the magical time of "after the war."

Two parallel images sum up this mental state. The first is a short anecdote from my grandfather. He had been relieving himself near a couple of supply trucks, probably of the famed Deuce-and-a-Half variety, when some enterprising Luftwaffe fliers buzzed the area and strafed the road. Diving under one of the trucks, my grandfather discovered to his mortification that he had literally been caught with his pants down.

If the possibility of taking a bullet while fulfilling the commandment of nature was an ever-present reminder of where he was, there was also a knowledge, so common in Allied troops at the time, that they were going to win the war and it might be soon. In one of the photos that I unearthed, my grandfather sits contentedly in the middle of a dirt road on a motorbike, probably taken from a German trooper. The note on the back of the photo reads:

> Say don't I look hot on that bike. Someone would think I was a State Trooper or something. That's a pretty good bike maybe I'll buy one when I come back [sic].

Although in France, the twentysomething American mindset could not be driven out easily, especially when the end of the war seemed so close. My grandfather had his portrait taken in Nancy, too, a portrait that still hangs in the upstairs hallway of my parents' house. With his soft, movie-star eyes and wistful gaze into the distance offset by the netted steel of his battle helmet and the barely-visible sergeant's chevrons on his left shoulder, the portrait is certainly flattering. We never learned if it was done by a Frenchman or by an enlisted photographer, but if anyone should desire to put a gallant, placid label on the war, he could do worse than this image.

Yet, the most enduring tale that my grandfather loved to tell involved Patton, who was the farthest thing from 'placid.' One particular day, my grandfather found himself somewhere on the road system outside of Metz. He had been riding in a jeep with his appointed driver. Along the side of the road, they spied a young French woman. This was nothing special in and of itself, as displaced refugees throughout the country had become the norm. What was different, though was that this particular woman appeared to be heavily pregnant and should clearly not be marooned on the side of the road.

Doing the chivalrous thing, my grandfather and his driver stopped, spoke to the woman with what little proficiency in the Gallic language they possessed, and managed to communicate that they could take her to a hospital. She agreed, they helped her into the jeep, and the small party made their way towards the nearest aid station.

'Say, don't I look hot on that bike'

It so happened that the route they were travelling was also being used by Patton on that particular day. As might be expected, Patton had not been sitting still during Third Army's confinement in western France. His inherently restless nature meant that he was constantly making his own frontline inspections and buzzing around the various units under his command. One of these outings brought him to an intersection with my grandfather's jeep.

Nancy, 1944

Patton, with an eye for anything not in perfect order, immediately recognized the non-regulation woman in the back of my grandfather's jeep and angrily pulled him over. Ivory-handled revolvers glistening in the sun, he demanded of my grandfather what this clearly unmilitary person was doing in a military transport. When my grandfather explained the situation, probably in a somewhat awestruck manner, Patton exploded. Under no circumstances would a civilian be permitted use of a military vehicle. She could be a spy! She could be a saboteur! At the very least, she was dead weight, and General Patton was not running an ambulance service or a maternity ward!

In front of his seething commander, the only thing my grandfather could do was escort the Frenchwoman out of his jeep to the roadside and be thankful that a tongue-lashing was the sole damage he incurred.

****

Patton's ornery disposition was certainly not helped by the fact that Metz stood unconquered directly to the north, a thorn in the side of American forces. Heavily fortified and ringed with an immense cordon of concrete bastions, the city's status hearkened back to the 17th century when siege engineers and star forts dictated Europe's balance of power. The forts presented a front quite similar to that of the Maginot line, and the foremost three still bore their French nomenclature: Fort St. Privat, Fort Jeanne d'Arc, and Fort Driant. Ambrose gives a description of the last of these:

The fort covered 355 acres of ground. It was surrounded by a twenty-meters-wide and ten-meters-deep moat, which in turn was surrounded by a twenty-meter band of barbed wire. It had living quarters for a garrison of 2,000. Its big guns rose from the earth, sniffed around, fired, and disappeared back into the earth. Most of the fortification was underground, along with food and ammunition supplies, aid stations and radio rooms, enough for a month of more of battle. The only way in was over a causeway.[6]

Fort Driant was like a medieval castle positioned underground, armed with modern weapons, and ready for a modern knight to try to take it. Patton, with his flair for romantic military history, and unable to concentrate his energy elsewhere, decided that he should be that knight. Metz's history as a strategic lynchpin, coupled with the promise of demonstrating that his men were unstoppable, made the prospect of batte here irresistible. Over Bradley's objections, in spite of the terrible casualties he would incur, Third Army must take the city.

The most obvious point of attack was Fort Driant, as it was sited comparatively far to the west of the city. September 27 and October 3 saw consecutive attacks on the fortifications, using a dizzying array of American weaponry. Flamethrowers, specialized bangalore torpodoes, tankdozers, TNT, napalm, and satchel charges were all pressed into service, along with the usual, brutally-concentrated applications of airstrikes and artillery. The assaults on Metz fell within the window of the 411th's stint as a field artillery unit, so my grandfather most likely found himself in support of these opening sallies.

Unforunately, these attacks stalled. The enormous quantity of high explosives that was poured on the German defenders proved unable to crack the reinforced-concrete nut that was Fort Driant. Some troops did manage to break into the concrete structure, but they soon found themselves fighting room-to-room in a grisly battle that resembled underground urban combat. Patton, rather than retreating, simply flung more men into the offensive. It was unthinkable that *his* men could fail to take a position. [5]

By October 13, however, this was exactly what appeared to have happened. With the units thrown into the attack having suffered nearly 50% casualties, and with the German defenders still in control of their concrete strongpoints, Patton had to relent. His memoirs simply, grumpily, note, "we decided to quit, as the operation was too costly." Temporarily, at least, the Third Army was thrown back into an unhappy stalemate. [7]

****

The southern wing of the Allied assault was hardly the only contingent of the Great Crusade that bled heavily in the autumn of '44. Farther to the north, fighting raged around and inside the city of Aachen, which was the historic seat of the

Holy Roman Empire, the crown jewel of the realms once held by Charlemagne, and an immensely valuable cultural prize in German tradition. Pinched from the north by the 30th Infantry Division and from the south by Collins's VII Corps, represented by the Big Red One, the German defenders of the city were forced into savage street fighting. The city, which had largely been reduced to rubble after extensive bombing sorties, was slowly cleared by door-to-door tactics that often involved using 155mm guns to pulverize defended structures at point-blank range. After a few weeks of mid-October fighting, including an almost-successful Nazi attempt to relieve the city with a column of Panzergrenadiers and Tiger tanks, the garrison commander of Aachen surrendered his forces on the 21st. Unlike the defenders of Metz earlier in the month, they could hold on no longer. They left to the Allies a charred rump of a city. Seemingly the only part that was spared was the famous cathedral and the tomb of Charlemagne.

  To the southeast of Aachen, a few weeks later, another contingent of Hodges's men found themselves in an altogether different type of struggle in the Hurtgen Forest. This woodland was vast, dark, and forboding. It stretched from the western banks of the Roer river in Germany east towards the Belgian border and had been fortified by the Wehrmacht in preparation for a general defense. Its densely packed trees made airpower and armor superiority effectively worthless. Any movement through the Hurtgen would have to done the old-fashioned way, on foot, by the infantry.

In spite of the these unappealing attributes, Hodges and the Allied brass had decided that these woods were significant in order to prevent a German flanking movement and to take a dam that could conceivably be blown to flood any eastern advance. So, the 28th Infantry, the Pennsylvania National Guard, was sent in on November 2.

The result was a prolonged bloodbath. German forces refused to give up their positions easily, and the initial infantry flung into the assault suffered terrible casualties. Although American units pushed far enough east to take the German town of Schmidt, they were soon met by a stiff, Panzer-led counterattack and had to retreat back towards their original lines. By November 9, the battle lines had stabilized, with the attacking units of the 28$^{th'}$ holding a position just slightly east of their starting point. For this ground World War I had effectively come again. Over next few months, an additional five divisions would be used in the Hurtgen forest and some 33,000 casualties would be taken. [8]

Patton, then, was in good company when he saw his grand offensive dissolve in the face of brutal casualties and unforgiving environmental obstacles. The men of Third Army were also far from alone in suffering from the ailments brought on by warfare in cold, dank, stationary conditions. Before the onset of the actual winter solstice, a combination of a lack of quality cold-weather gear and entrenchments that were not conducive to maintaining warmth hit frontline troops hard.

Probably the worst and most prevalent malady was trench foot, that medical incubus that always seems to plague massed troop formations. Caused during frigid conditions by keeping the feet and boots soaked in water for sustained periods of time, trench foot is described grimly by Ambrose:

> First a man lost his toenails. His feet turned white, then purple, finally black. A serious case of trench foot made walking impossible. Many men lost their toes, some had to have their feet amputated. If gangrene set in, the doctors had to amputate the lower leg . [9]

Over 20,000 men were taken out of action because of trench foot in the months of November and December alone. Many more exhibited symptoms that were not severe enough to remove them from the line. My grandfather most likely fell into this latter category. Thankfully, his condition never advanced past the first sentence in Ambrose's sober progression, as he kept his toenails, albeit in a badly damaged and warped state that remained a nuisance for the rest of his life. It became a matter of family conjecture that the real reason for this was frostbite incurred during December, but I am inclined to chalk up this explanation to a lack of knowledge among us civilians about the real diseases of the battlefield. [10]

As November began, in spite of a dawning and depressing realization that the war would probably continue for at least several more months, Patton remained resolute in his objective of capturing the fortified jewel that was Metz. Of course, because of a combination of the dreary weather and relentless bombardment, the city and its environs were more of a brown morass than a jewel. Nevertheless, it still represented a substantial obstacle that lay between Third Army and the promise of decisively piercing the German border.

After the debacle at Fort Driant in October, Patton and his tacticians had discarded the idea of flinging men in a direct assault at Metz. For a second stab at taking the city, the plan would instead be a wide envelopment. With plenty of firepower, including the guns of the 411th at Pont-à-Mousson, securing the Moselle River just to the west of Metz, some nine divisions would advance on a broad front and cut the city off from the main German line. In particular, the 90th and 95th Divisions would swing south, linking up behind Metz with the northbound 5th.

After yet another massive preliminary bombardment by Jimmy Doolittle's fliers, the offensive got underway on November 8. Over the next week, as the autumn rains turned to sleet, bastion after bastion fell. Third Army was mobile again, and Patton, in spite of the rotten weather, was having a jolly time of it. He was exuberant in proclaiming the advance of the 90th over the Moselle an "epic assault." He delightedly reported on November 12 that he had "never seen so many dead Germans." Even when he accidentally burned down Eisenhower's hotel while attempting to light a fire in the visiting commander's room, this was shrugged off as an "amusing incident." [13]

All told, encirclement and demolitions exerience gained from the earlier assaults proved more able to reduce concrete strongpoints than suicidal frontal attacks. It also certainly helped that many of the German defenders proved to be so-called *halb-soldaten*, "half-soldiers." Germany had reached the bottom of its manpower barrel, and the Wehrmacht could no longer spend the lives of blond-haired, blue-eyed young men with the same reckless abandon that it had five years earlier.

It is worth noting that the Nazi forces were not alone in feeling the side-effects of high casualties. As easy as it is to fall into the trap of mentally separating the German and American combatants and automatically assigning the latter to an axiomatically higher level of martial ability, the Wehrmacht's reliance by 1944 on old men, teenagers, and walking-wounded was similar to the American dependence on vast streams of replacements. The latter of these were kids barely out of high school or men who were previously considered too "physically imperfect" to serve. They were expected to step in and seamlessly replicate the combat acumen of veterans seasoned by live fire. They were needed because every single American division in the European theater was understrength.

Of course, no amount of stateside or rear-area training could ever be adequate preparation for the chaos of the front lines, and combat infantry outfits, because of their inherently higher casualty rates, were where replacements were most needed. Notwithstanding this fact, replacement GI's bound for regiments that were online found themselves thrown almost immediately into combat. If they lasted a few days, that was usually enough to earn them veteran status. As Ambrose puts it:

> Training was critical to getting the men into physical condition, to obey orders, to use their weaopns, to work effectively with hand signals and radios, and more. It could not teach men how to lie helpless under a shower of shrapnel in a field crosscrossed by machine-gune fire. They just had to do it, and in doing it they joined a unique group of men who have experienced what the rest of us cannot imagine. [12]

Such a rapid transformation over the course of a single engagement is a sobering timeline when viewed from a civilian perspective. Of all the professions on earth, only the practice of arms allows its student to graduate to master status after a week, or a day, or a matter of hours. The poetic nature of this is just as evident as its violent simplicity. If the replacement survives, he gains a status unknown to the way of life he just left; he becomes a veteran. If he does not survive, it is because he could not or did not learn what was needed to ascend, often through no fault of his own.

How this transformation occurs is a fascinating question. Such a rapid acquisition of the knowledge of brutality, of how to kill effectively and of how to stay alive when others are trying to kill you, must have a profound impact on any man's psyche. Unlike the original members of the Allied armies in North Africa and Sicily, the men who were encountering combat for the first time were doing so against the 'primary' enemy, Germany, not against Vichy French or Italian proxy opponents. It is tempting to think that the men who were veterans by November 1944, those who were still left from the earlier fighting, had had a chance to gradually develop their feelings for the enemy, to gradually come to grips with their status on the line.

But even if this is not true, could it be that the first *hate* for the enemy would begin to show after a man survived a week on the line, after he had learned what he needed to do to survive in this campaign? And, if so, was this also a time when he would first feel his humanity tugging away from him and would face the possibility of losing the *citizen* part of the name *citizen-soldier*?

AAA, artillery, and even armored formations did not experience the same attrition rates as rifle companies. My grandfather, five months into his tour, could be reasonably considered a veteran, but, thankfully, he never had to cope with the experience of being a replacement. What transformative process did he undergo, then? In what manner was his citizen status eroded as the days under fire wore on?

****

Metz officially surrendered on November 22, although it would be another few weeks before all the German forces in the surrounding forts were neutralized. Still, the victory was sufficiently complete for Patton to celebrate his subordinates who had led the main columns of the attack. They warranted fanfare from one of Third Army's bands. Patton, of course, gave himself a more boisterous reward in the form of a siren-blaring entrance into Metz in his personal jeep. [11]

With the capture of Metz, the month of November ended with Third Army pressing firmly against the German border. The advance had been significantly less rapid than anticipated - the armored drive had not come close to rapidly mounting the Rhine and knifing through the German heartland. For the 411th, who were still in position at Pont-à-Mousson, the month had been less of a drive than a stationary struggle. For all the enormous losses that the Luftwaffe had incurred, it was still able to mount regular sorties against Allied supply lines across the Moselle, and friendly planes simply could not patrol everywhere at once. So, the AAA squatted, fired, and waited.

The next phase for Patton's troops would be to puncture a definite hole in the fortifications that guarded the

French-German, the *Westwall*. Also known as the 'Siegfried Line,' after the Wagnerian hero, Patton had famously scoffed at it earlier in the year. That, however, was before his columns had bogged down in mud and concrete outside of Metz. The Siegfried Line, as the Nazi response to the Maginot Line, was dilapidated in many spots and manned by what sub-par, *halb-soldaten* were available in the west. But, it was still viciously fortified with thousands of bunkers, well-camouflaged, and sited to allow the best firing positions possible against any Allied attack. Taking it was no guaranteed business. [14]

    This was the immediate problem that Third Army was attempting to solve as the winter solstice approached. However, developments further north would require a change of plans in the ensuing weeks.

December

As December opened, Third Army was enacting the initial phases of its strike across the Saar river, through the Westwall, and into southern Germany. The offensive, planned in close coordination with the Air Corps, was designed to bring Patton's men to that most formidable natural barrier, the Rhine, by December 19. From there, gasoline limitations notwithstanding, they could roam free in the enemy's backfield. Two problems, however, prevented the immediate success of this maneuver.

The first of these was the terrible weather. Grey skies and mud were still the order of the day, as were the reduced mobility and constraints on aircover that they brought. Of this, Patton had had enough. In a famous story recounted by Patton's deputy chief of staff, future-General Paul Harkins, the chaplain of the Third Army was summoned to headquarters on December 14:

> *General Patton*: 'Chaplain, I want you to publish a prayer for good weather. I'm tired of these soldiers having to fight mud and floods as well as Germans. See if we can't get God to work on our side.'
>
> *Chaplain O'Neill*: 'Sir, it's going to take a pretty thick rug for that kind of praying.'
>
> *General Patton*: 'I don't care if it takes the flying carpet. I want the praying done.'

Chaplain O'Neill: 'Yes, sir. May I say, General, that it usually isn't a customary thing among men of my profession to pray for clear weather to kill fellow men.'

General Patton: 'Chaplain, are you teaching me theology or are you the Chaplain of the Third Army? I want a prayer.'

Out of this exchange emerged the following prayer:

Almighty and most merciful Father, we humbly beseech Thee, of Thy great goodness, to restrain these immoderate rains with which we have had to contend. Grant us fair weather for Battle. Graciously hearken to us as soldiers who call upon Thee that, armed with Thy power, we may advance from victory to victory, and crush the oppression and wickedness of our enemies, and establish Thy justice among men and nations. Amen. [1]

The nature of the language used here is strikingly forceful for a Christian prayer, especially from the lens of a modern perspective. It raises the question of how the typical soldier on the front lines viewed religion. Certainly, Patton was an anomaly; men as profane and generally cold-blooded as he was are rarely so devout. Yet, the faith of Third Army's commander was hardly odd in an era where only the outliers of society did not, at least outwardly, believe in God. What is perhaps a more telling and relevant question that could be fairly posed by the modern civilian would be, given an army of millions of mostly Judeo-Christian men, how is the call to peace of those religions reconciled with the bloodthirsty task in which their practitioners found themselves embroiled during the wartime years? Must there not be a paradox at work, or, worse yet, a mark of hypocrisy? Brief observations of modern news stories indicate that this is a perfectly relevant issue.

Most men on the frontlines had, one way or another, reconciled the killing of other men with their religious beliefs. As Ambrose puts it, it was difficult to find "that rare creature, an atheist in a foxhole." [2] It would be easy enough to dismiss the combination of a belief in peaceful Christianity and a willingness to slay the enemy if most frontline troops who held such views were like Patton, that is, career soldiers, bred for war. Old Blood 'n Guts was remarkable, though, because he was different. Most men had a home life they would rather return to. Most men would not be merrily singing 'Noel, Noel, what a night to give the Nazis hell' on Christmas Eve if they had any other choice. [3] Most men were civilians at heart who had been thrust into an unenviable situation.

Perhaps, then, these massed American legions simply represented an example of the old Latin proverb, *Si Vis Pacem, Para Bellum*: "If you would have peace, prepare for war." Perhaps, on some primordial level, a cross-section of America and her Allies was able to reconcile that seeming-paradox of axiomatic peace versus necessary destruction in a mass movement that consisted of pure action. In doing so, they would have done a better job of cutting the Gordian knot of pacifist worrying that always accompanies questions about just war than any number of ponderous arguments by armchair philosophers could ever do. Perhaps being thrust into the heart of the action, when death, violence, and camaraderie become the norm, acts as a burst of fresh air to clear out philosophical conundrums that are insolvable under more tranquil circumstances.

Or, perhaps, being in a foxhole simply made men scared and made them cling to their faith more strongly than they would have done if they were not in mortal peril? Ernie Pyle makes a sideways comment to this effect, noting that chaplains on troop transports making their way across the Atlantic reported that "church attendance among the troops went up noticeably after we sailed, and continued to rise as we approached submarine waters." [4] Yet, I cannot reconcile this view with what I grew to know about my grandfather. Even after the guns had long gone silent, his religious devotion was second to none, and it was not caused by fear of any man or army. It is hard to imagine that most of his comrades were any different.

In the final account, it is far easier for a person who has never known battle to argue against the existence of a just reason for killing. If an engagement can be the cause of a sharpening of the perceptory senses, why can it not also be the cause of a heigtening of an understanding of the fundamental laws of being?

At any rate, after Patton's requested prayer was distributed to Third Army a week later, the weather cleared, and Allied air superiority was reestablished.

****

The second item that prevented Patton from making a major breakthrough was not so easily removed. On December 16, just a few days before Third Army believed it could achieve the close bank of the Rhine, the last major German offensive on the Western Front kicked off to the north. Two entire Panzer Armies, the 5th and the 6th, were hurled against American forces in Luxembourg and Belgium, respectively. Hitler's objective? To resurrect the blitzkrieg, punch through to the crucial ports of the North Sea and English Channel, and drive the Allies back into the water. The targets of the initial onslaught were to be the members of Courtney Hodges's First Army.

The results of the first 24 hours of the assault were mixed. The 6th Panzer Army in the north ran out of steam fairly quickly in the face of a furious concentration of American artillery. Just to the south, however, where the 5th and 6th Armies overlapped, German troops broke through rapidly in the direction of St. Vith. American forces there fled west in a winding, disheveled column that resembled the German exodus from Normandy four months earlier.

Further south, along the Luxembourg border and the main front of the 5th Army, Wehrmacht successes were still striking, though less spectacular. Having received reinforcements that the German high command shuttled from the faltering attack in the north, the 5th found itself facing a long, thin line of mostly inexperienced and battered troops along the breadth of Luxembourg. These included the 28th Division, which was recuperating after its ordeal in the Hurtgen. Its 112th, 110th, and 109th regiments were responsible for defending the border of the entire country.

In spite of their numerical paucity, the overstretched lines of the 28th were nonetheless able to offer respectable resistance to the advancing German forces. The 110th particularly distinguished itself, holding the center of the line. The unit fought until it was effectively wiped out, taking 2,500 casualties and losing 60 tanks, absurd numbers for a single regiment. In doing so, the spearhead of the 5th Army that was to zip through Luxembourg and capture the critical town of Bastogne was delayed. [5]

Because of this holdup, Eisenhower and the Allied command could play one of the cards they had been keeping in reserve. The 82nd and 101st Airborne, probably as exhausted after the brutal fighting in the Netherlands as the 28th Infantry was after its stint in the Hurtgen, had been in the process of refitting and reequipping themselves for combat when the German offensive kicked off. In spite of their tired condition, the paratroopers were designated as a key component of the official Strategic Reserve. So, eastwards they marched, picking up ammunition as they went from the panicked columns fleeing the other way. Gavin's 82nd was headed in the direction of Werbomont and Spa, near the German border, while the 101st was bound for the more famous destination of Bastogne. There, they would dig in and grimly wait for the approaching Wehrmacht. [6]

    This was the situation as of December 19. At the same time, a couple of hours to the southwest, Ike convened a council of war at the city of Verdun, site of the famously bloody Great War battle. Among the officers present were Bradley and, of course, Patton, who had already mapped out multiple plans for a counterattack with his staff. A counterattack by Third Army was exactly what Eisenhower was looking for. He asked for an assualt to the north against the exposed southern flank of the Wehrmacht within six days. Patton shot back that he would do it within three, by the 23rd. The attack, which actually got off on the 22nd, would be the most impressive left-turn of the war.

    So, as the 101st, under General Anthony McAuliffe, prepared itself in Bastogne for a Christmas under siege, Third Army gathered its energy and redirected its march northwards. The initial attack would consist of the divisions of the III Corps, the 26th and 80th Infantry and the 4th Armored, a powerful force in its own right. As wheeling these units, a substantial portion of Third Army, almost 90 degrees from their initial axis of attack was a move fraught with potential danger, Patton arrived in Luxembourg on the morning of the 20th to personally oversee developments. Speed, as always, would need to be the hallmark of the campaign.

Keeping the vehicular services running

The entirety of the Third Army did not participate in the move, of course. There was too much ground to cover along its original front to uproot the whole force at once, even considering that First Army's VIII Corps, including the troops under siege in Bastogne, was absorbed into Patton's command and that Seventh Army to the south would chip in and help defend some of Third Army's territory.

Another unit that found itself left out of the drive northwards was the 411th. The battalion had moved forward to the newly-captured positions at Metz on December 6, but that would be the extent of its repositioning. Through Christmas, through the Bulge campaign, through the cold European winter of 1944-45, my grandfather and his comrades would remain parked on the vital supply routes near the Moselle and blaze away at German raiders.

Although not glamorous and not noted by the history books, tt was certainly a job that needed doing.The Luftwaffe, although still a shadow of its former self and possessed of nowhere near the power of the Allied air forces, had managed to regroup to the point where it could offer some support to the Panzer armies on the ground. No small part of this support was in the form of rear-area bombing, which brought AAA units straight into the limelight.

The 411th was no exception. During the course of the Bulge campaign, the battalion racked up 15 confirmed kills, one of the most impressive tallies since August. D Battery got their fair share, accounting for nine aircraft. These were mostly Me-109's, the workhorse German fighters. The battalion could also claim a Focke-Wolfe 190, an Me-110, a Ju-88, and a medium bomber, an He-111, quite a diverse tally for guns relying on undirected flak. Incidentally, a newfangled invention called the 'proximity fuse' was just finding its way into use by ground-to-ground artillery. Although it made Allied firepower far more accurate (German soldiers were convinced it could use the earth's magnetic field to make a shell explode at the perfect spot), the new fuse was a weapon that had not yet made the rounds among the antiair gunners. Perhaps in the next war there would be something for them. [7]

Advances in weaponry aside, my grandfather's role as an NCO in the motorpool meant that he was rarely on the firing line when the battery's guns were engaged. In spite of this, he still would speak of them reverently, like an English lord might speak of thoroughbred warhorses. Just as an infantryman was (and is) taught to regard his rifle as his life, anti-aircraft artillerists could regard their ack-ack guns as the sinews of war. They were the reason the battalion existed, and every surrounding structure in the unit was there to support them. Their successes were the battalion's successes, their kills, the battalion's kills.

Between active ground-based anti-aircraft and ever-active American airmen, supply lines for Third Army's pivot northwards were kept open. There would be no pinching of gasoline and ammunition reserves as there had been in the fall: Patton would have no need to rage against a lack of martial means.

****

In spite of an unthreatened supply situation, Third Army's charge northwards did not go as smoothly as Patton would have preferred. The weather that had cleared during the earlier offensive in the aftermath of Patton's prayer drive had since soured again and only permitted Allied air cover to reemerge as Christmas Eve approached. Still, even with renewed support from the skies, the Shermans of 4th Armored made precious little progress in the face of deep snow and stubborn resistance. Patton found himself issuing an uncharacteristic apology to Ike for the delay. To make matters worse, no help would come from Monty's forces in the north. Originally slated to crash into the northern end of the German Bulge, the British commander (now also boasting operational control over a number of American units, including Hodges's First Army) decided that more time was needed to rest and refit his men before beginning a concerted counterstroke.

In the midst of all of this, the Bulge had congealed, and the Wehrmacht's progress had ground to a halt. Pockets of American resistance sucked in vital German manpower that could be have been better used at the tip of the spearhead. Of these pockets that still survived, the most prominent was the 101st, still stuck in Bastogne on an unhappy Christmas Day.

Three days prior, an officer from the Panzer Lehr Division, one of the elements of the corps-sized force that faced the surrounded 101st, had made his way into the cordon around Bastogne. Demanding an 'honorable surrender' from McAuliffe, he recieved the famously terse rejoinder, 'Nuts.' After the message was translated into an expression that the bewildered German could understand ('Go to Hell'), the officer returned to his unit, and the attack began anew. [8]

The type of formation that would answer a Nazi demand with homespun American irreverence while surrounded, outnumbered three-to-one, freezing, and half-starving was one that Patton would want to save. Although Third Army was not able to reach this milestone by Christmas, they proved luckier the day after. On December 26th, the 37th Armored Battalion, a detachment of the 4th Armored under Creighton Abrams (future eponym of the M1 Abrams tank), joined up with the southern sector of the 101st. The region around Bastogne would not be fully relieved until some weeks later, but the paratroopers had held out.

Third Army, then, was on the move. Montgomery was still stuck in position with the First and Ninth Armies, unable or unwilling to attack south and east. Troops on both sides were freezing and hungry. Allied forces could, as always, count on enormous artillery barrages, the ever-advancing Soviets on the other side of Europe (who had now arrived in the northern Balkans), and, when there was clear weather, the vanquishing angels of the air forces. The Wehrmacht, though, could take little solace in anything. Their grand offensive, promised by Hitler to turn the tide of the war in the West, had become merely a static geographic anomaly that jutted awkwardly into Belgium. [9]

The two sides had vastly different outlooks for the future. But, both celebrated Christmas and New Year's in the shadow of death. Trees bedecked with tinsel and appropriated sausages and champagne made the frigid temperatures more bearable, and the occasional carol would break the winter silence, but they could not detract from the somber atmosphere – the famous Christmas truces of the

Great War are not so easily discerned in the annals of 1944. In the 411th, D Battery scored an Me-109 on Christmas Eve; B Battery got a Focke-Wolfe flier on Christmas Day. It was par for the course: 'Noel, Noel, what a night to give the Nazis hell.' [10]

****

In his memoirs, Patton tends to make frequent matter-of-fact remarks about subjects that are not tactically or stragetically relevant in nature. One of these appears during his recollections of Christmas day during the drive north:

> It is to the great credit of the Quartermaster Corps that on this Christmas Day every soldier had turkey; those in the front had turkey sandwiches and the rest, hot turkey. I know of no army in the world except the American which could have done such a thing. The men were surprisingly cheerful. [11]

Apart from the facts that the troops shivering in isolated outposts like Bastogne would probably have only enjoyed cold K-rations and that, in general, the army supply services deserved a pat on the back for such an achievement of distribution, the other point of Patton's observation that is particularly interesting is the precise foodstuff that he mentions: turkey. The simile "as American as" can be applied to many things, and a turkey dinner, concocted out of the bird that very nearly became a national emblem, is certainly one of those things.

For most Americans, turkey is a profoundly evocative food. Outside of lunchmeat, most of us only eat it perhaps once or twice a year at Thanksgiving and Christmas. It has an immediate association with specific people, cherished places, and treasured memories. It cuts to the heart of what food truly is, a substance that goes far beyond intertwined globs of protein, fats, and carbohydrates necessary to maintain human life.

My family always placed a great deal of importance on the culinary aspect of the two late-year holidays. It was not that we valued the act of eating or cooking over the five of us being together. Rather, the food itself was a catalyst for bringing joy to the day. There was always an emphasis that was placed on ensuring that everything was scratch-made: the pies, the stuffing, the breads would all be created from their constituent ingredients. The family would come together to both create and consume a one-of-a-kind, fleeting piece of art that only we could share.

Perhaps the most attractive point about our art was its fundamental imperfections. Our family videos show the full glory of a turkey that was sliced not for aesthetic appeal, but for the purposes of making it easy to distribute; of a gravy dish and a bowl of mashed potatoes that would rapidly become smeared over with runoff from the sides; and of my grandfather gleefully directing forkfuls of a jagged and irregular (but homemade!) apple pie into the mouth of his grandson, murmuring, 'Boy, that's a good one, isn't it?' The point was not to create a masterpiece in the food itself - the food was a nutritive expression of love, and only dehomogenization could elevate it above being nothing more than something to eat.

In the movie *Burnt*, Bradley Cooper's character, a chef, offers a commentary on fast food. The problem, as he sees it, with Burger King and McDonald's, is not that the food served there is hypercaloric and unhealthy - the same could be said of the best French cooking. The problem is that it is mass-produced and uniform. It cannot act as the vessel of a culinary art because four ounces of ground beef, salt, pepper, lettuce, tomato, onion, special sauce, and a bun, shaped into a circle of a specific radius, cooked in a specific fat at a specific temperature for a specific time and served in a specific type of paper must, by necessity, always turn out the same.

In and of itself, there is nothing wrong with this. But, in the absence of variation, a major source of joy and art is lost. Sameness can be the enemy of both. It was the imperfections in our family's meal that rendered it a celebration of the kind of exploration that can be enjoyed when a group is at peace.

Napoleon's famous maxim that an army marches on its stomach is every bit as true now as it was in his Russian campaign, just as it was true in the Second World War. Logistics, both nutritional and otherwise, will always have a large say in the effectiveness of any fighting force. But, to what extent is it sufficient to merely ensure that combat troops are fed a diet sufficient in nutrient content? Is there not something missing if prepackaged, scientifically-measured bags of food are the only form of sustenance for a soldier? Perhaps this is especially true for the citizen-soldier. Just as the hardships of war deprive him of many of the other facets of civilian life that are considered to be cornerstones of a peaceful existence, the ability to enjoy an imperfect-yet-artistically-prepared meal is one more item that must be abandoned on the front lines.

    Third Army's turkey procurement ability, then, may be viewed as a recognition that a steady diet of K-rations would not meet a deeper human requirement for food. As Patton said, the American soldier was the only one in the world who could have enjoyed such a treat for his holiday meal. Perhaps that has something to do with the uniqueness of the American citizen-soldier, a uniqueness that, on some level, his broader supply service understood.

January-April

New Year's Day 1945 dawned on a landscape that was still frozen in the throes of war, the Bulge still stubbornly jutting into the American lines in Belgium like an icy bodkin embedded in a sheet of chainmail. Per his flair for the dramatic, Patton issued a proclamation to inaugurate the year:

> From the bloody corridor at Avranches, to Brest, thence across France to the Saar, over the Saar into Germany, and now on to Bastogne, your record has been one of continuous victory...
> My New Year wish and sure conviction for you is that, under the protection of Almighy God and the inspired leadership of our President and the High Command, you will continue your victorious course to the end that tyranny and vice shall be eliminated, our dead comrades avenged, and peace restored to a war-weary world.
> In closing, I can find no fitter expression for my feelings than to apply to you the immortal words spoken by General Scott at Chapultepec when he said: "Brave rifles, veterans, you have been baptized in fire and blood and have come out steel." [1]

Although it is unlikely that anyone else on the line was reminded of the victorious anabasis that was the Mexican

A Germanic Winter

War on this particular morning, Third Army certainly had some reason to feel that the momentum was on their side. Within a week, the Wehrmacht received permission from Hitler to pull back to the Westwall. Eight days later, on January 16, after a bitterly cold yet hotly-contested advance, First Army's counterattack met up with the tip of Patton's spear at Houffalize. And, although Bradley had to contain his fury at a gut-wrenchingly awkward Montgomery press conference in which the British commander breezily took credit for the whole battle ('As soon as I saw what was happening I took certain steps myself to ensure... they [the Germans] would certainly not get over that river'), the fact remained that the offensive could soon be resumed. The certification that the 101st sardonically gave to Bastogne could be applied to the whole Allied line: 'Kraut disinfected.' [2]

The early days of January were no less interesting for the 411th, beginning right on New Years Day. Their bivouac around Metz erupted around 9 AM in a swarm of vengeful Me-109's. Unusually for an AA unit, the 411th, not the infrastructure around it, was reported by the day's AAR as the target of the raiders.

Shortly after the fracas began, D Battery found their radar station disabled by a solitary 50-caliber round that had punctured the magnetron. Without radar coverage, the battery found itself fighting off 16 Messerschmitts which came roaring in at a strafing altitude of less than 100 feet, guns blazing. The attack lasted perhaps ten excruciating minutes and cost the Luftwaffe three of their fliers. Shockingly, no casualties were reported among the battery.

Elsewhere in the battalion, other batteries were not so fortunate. A major theme that had arisen in First Army's sector earlier in the Bulge campaign was the confusion and panic that German infiltrators, disguised as Allied personnel, could inflict. That confusion had been on the ground; it turned out that similar disorder could be created in the air using the same techniques. Over the course of the war's airborne engagements, the Luftwaffe had recovered a number of American Mustangs. Repurposing them with German markings and German pilots, they were deployed alongside other squadrons. As might be expected, this aerial infiltration presented a great difficulty for AA gunners. In the battle above Metz, distinguishing friend from foe became a tall order; even the destruction of the 411th's radar was originally thought to be a friendly fire incident.

The worst damage of the raid, due to a combination of surprise and deception, was done in the sectors of neighboring batteries. Some 14 P-47's parked on a nearby airstrip were destroyed, and the AAR reports mutedly that there "were a number of personnel casualties of the engineers and Air Corps." For one 24-hour period, this was quite a toll for the units defending a single location.

Nevertheless, over the succeeding days, the force of the German raids steadily tapered off, and the focus of the battalion turned to other matters. In addition to frequent and upbeat reports of the presence of friendly bomber flights, there was also a curious incident on January 6 involving D Battery. That evening, two explosions, neither causing any damage or casualties, had rocked an area immediately adjacent to D Battery's position. Upon investigation, an apparently drunk civilian was found next to a shack which was being used to store ordnance. He quickly confessed to having been the instigator, although the soldiers who interviewed him were convinced he was only "feigning" his inebriation.

The next morning, when an MP did a more thorough search of the area, a boy was found hiding out in possession of a number of American and German hand grenades. All things considered, it appears that a French g*arçon* found a delightful cache of particularly noisy fireworks and decided to set them off, forcing, presumably, his father to act out the role of a drunken buffoon to redirect potential retribution away from his son. No more was said of the incident in Army records.³

At any rate, the fact that a drama like this could play out without any intervening bloodshed was a bellwether of coming changes. As the Third Army finished up its campaign in the Bulge, its center-of-mass had shifted slowly northwards, in the direction of Luxembourg and Belgium and away from Metz. By the time the Army's great clockwise pivot had finished, the 411th was preparing to decamp to rejoin the main body of troops. The battalion pulled into the town of Eich, Luxembourg, a suburb slightly north of the tiny country's capital, on February 5. There they would remain for the rest of the month without enough action to warrant a confirmed kill.⁴

****

For the combat infantry, though, the second month of 1945 was not nearly so calm. The freezing temperatures of the early winter had risen just enough to turn fields of stark-white snow into piles of thawed mud. In the face of this unenviable muck, the Allied offensive resumed the eastward course that it had had to abandon to deal with the Bulge.

In the south, between Strasbourg and the Swiss border, a massive reduction of the so-called "Colmar pocket" of German resistance sucked in the 6th Army Group. A mirror image of the fighting done by Bradley's 12th in puncturing the Bulge, the contest around Colmar would take the better part of two months. It was only by arguing vociferously that Patton and Bradley managed to keep their divisions from being diverted into this vortex.

To the north of Third Army, in Monty's sector, the British Second, Canadian First, and American Ninth Armies readied a push over the Roer River that would finally restore some movement to a sector that had been largely sedentary since the disaster that was Market Garden. The ultimate objective was the Rhine, a bit more than 20 miles east of the Roer, and the Ruhr beyond it. There lay the German industrial heartland.

Third Army itself, sandwiched in the middle of the Allied effort, was also targeting the Rhine. To do so, however, it would have to finally close with the Westwall, which circumstances had compelled Patton to avoid earlier.

The state of German fortifications along their formidable defensive line varied substantially from point to point. In some locales, Patton's assessment of the rows of concrete bunkers and tank traps as "monument[s] to the stupidity of man" were proven correct when the only troops the Wehrmacht could muster to garrison these structures were starving formations desperate to surrender. Elsewhere, resistance was much fiercer when the German defenders decided to stand their ground.

In spite of the variable porousness of the defenses, every location on the Siegfried Line that faced the Third Army was overrun in a matter of weeks – Hitler's concrete fortress had been breached. With more than a bit of self-vindication on the efficacy of forwardly moving infantry and armor, Patton lectured in his memoirs:

> Pacifists would do well to study the Siegfried and Maginot Lines, remembering that these defenses were forced... and that, by the same token, the mighty seas which are alleged to defend us can also be circumvented by a resolute and ingenious opponent. In war, the only sure defense is offense, and the efficiency of offense depends on the warlike souls of those conducting it. [7]

After the great German ring of concrete had been punctured, the cities that lay between it and the Rhine fell in swift succession; within a month, Trier, Bitburg, Coblenz, and Andernach had all been taken. By March 13, VIII Corps, the spearhead of the original northbound Bulge offensive, was sitting just south of Coblenz on the west bank of the Rhine, poised to swoop across at the first chance it got. The unit had made this progress in only 41 days. XII Corps, which had the honor of entering Trier, had only needed 11 days to accomplish its objective. Even in an era of mechanization, these were exceptionally quick maneuvers. [5, 6, 8]

Progress was being made elsewhere along the Allied front, as well. Hodges's Army had forced a bridgehead over the Rhine back on March 7 in Remagen, northwest of Coblenz. An armored detachment had succeded in capturing the city's Ludendorff Bridge after a failed German demolition attempt. Although the Wehrmacht was eventually able to knock the crossing out by a combination of airstrikes and heavy artillery fire, First Army's engineers had, in the interim, bought themselves enough time on the eastern bank of the river to produce an array of other bridges. On March 19, Eisenhower ordered nine divisions over these new corridors in Caesaraean style. [9]

Back in the south, Patton would not be outdone. Third Army's stunning capture of German city after German city wrapped up on March 22, finishing what became known as the Palatinate campaign, named after a region that possessed a particularly rich heritage as an electorate of the long-defunct Holy Roman Empire. It was appropriate that Patton, with his flair for reinvigorating historical meaning, was the one to take a sector with such deep Germanic heritage.

Historical significance aside, Darmstadt, Mainz, Worms, Mannheim, and Heidlberg were now in imminent danger, protected only by the Rhine and whatever skeletal force the Wehrmacht could scrape together to provide for their defense. It would not be enough. The 5th Infantry, representing XII Corps, stealthily jumped across at a point south of Mainz at 11:30 PM on the 22nd. Of six battalions that made it across by daybreak, only twenty-eight casualties were taken – German resistance was in the process of disintegrating, yet again. This time, there would be no revitalizing counteroffensive.

Patton himself made the trek across the river on the 24th, stopping to urinate in the water on his way across. He also made a point to act out a modernized scene from the life of Scipio Africanus (he intentionally tripped upon arriving on the eastern bank of the Rhine, rising with a dramatized 'I see in my hands the soil of Germany') and to insist to his Corps commanders, each in turn, that *his* Corps be the first to reach the Army's rally point. Incidentally, the British forces up north had also crossed the Rhine on this day in a grand and boisterous operation that saw the unheralded XVIII Airborne Corps carry out a drop on the far side of the river. Monty's assault also saw a visiting Winston Churchill relieve himself in the ancient waterway with gleeful vengeance – evidently, this was a popular gesture. [10, 11, 12, 13]

The 411th, of course, did not get to experience the heady movement at the front. The battalion did, however, officially arrive on German soil on March 26, just outside of Saarbug, assuredly glad that the Luftwaffe had been diminished enough to render their jobs a good deal less dangerous. There were still occasional air raids to fight off, and Hitler's threats of jet aircraft coming to rescue the Reich still hung in the ether, but, the months of early spring in 1945 saw few air-to-ground engagements to speak of.

What the 411th did share in common with the rest of Third Army, though, was an enormous increase in mobility. With German resistance reaching almost negligible levels by late March, the battalion found itself changing locales at nearly the same rate as it did during the previous August on its initial romp through France. By the first day in April, Easter Sunday, it had reached the opposite bank of the Rhine. In the process, due in no small part to both the depleted Luftwaffe and excellent weather conditions for American fliers, the battalion found itself impressed as a de facto supply unit:

> In addition to their primary, twenty-four-hou-per-day mission of furnishing anti-aircraft protection for critical Third U.S. Army installations, these units hauled vitally needed gasoline and personal [sic] reinforcements to forward armored and infantry elements during the critical period of operations... The skillful manner in which they were accomplished, often under difficult conditions... are in keeping with the highest traditions of the service. [14]

A constant flow of supplies to the front was necessary because an entirely new phase of the war had opened up. The dash across France before the quagmire around Metz had been an exciting time in the history of American armored warfare. Third Army's advance on the eastern side of the Rhine that kicked off at the beginning of April was something else entirely. The great autobahn highways that were to allow Hitler's war machine to effortlessly shuttle mechanized units across the country were now used as vast conveyor belts that delivered division after division into the heart of the Reich. The vast rural fields that represented the heartland of the master race now became open terrain which American infantry and armor could effortlessly cross, unhindered by whatever broken and demoralized Wehrmacht units still existed in the German south.

The reasonable sense that victory was assured permeated through the ranks at all levels. As one soldier put it, 'You get the feeling that the army is an immense flood pouring over the countryside... You move with the tide, and it carries you along in an almost effortless fashion.' In many cases, the sole resistance that Nazi forces could offer were obstacles that came to be called 'sixty-one roadblocks,' named for the fact that American soldiers would laugh at them for sixty minutes and demolish them one minute later.

The token German forces left did nothing to suggest they were anything other than helpless. On at least one occastion, a rear-area section of the Third Army stumbled upon a bloc of German generals, idly waiting for someone to come along and tell them that their war was over. They duly got their wish.

Still, exhaustion was rampant in Third Army, as April marked the fourth straight month of constant offensive action. There were perpetually cases of self-inflicted wounds, raising Patton's ever-simmering ire. The infuriated general "would use about three lines of choice profanity and state that, by wounding himself, he [the soldier] not only showed he was a coward, but also added to the labor and risk of the brave men who did not use this means of getting out of battle." As always, though, the broadest section of the army, tired and pining for home as they were, kept moving eastward. [15, 16, 17]

****

By April 21, it was clear to all sane observers that Germany was finished. Third Army had overrun Nuremberg, Erfurt, and Weimar, which had given its name to the ill-fated post-Great-War German government. To the north, Hodges had taken Leipzig, and Montgomery had finally flushed out the Netherlands on his way towards the old Danish border.

The Allied high command, however, was still worried about repeating the error in judgment that led to the debacle of the Bulge. The chief concern that lurked in the back of their minds was that of an 'Alpine Redoubt,' a last-ditch stronghold in the Bavarian Alps where Hitler could entrench himself and several thousand die-hard SS troops and fight a guerilla war for years. Hindsight being what it is, such a supposition on the part of Eisenhower and his peers seems foolish. There was never sufficient manpower or defensive armaments poured into the mountains to sustain this kind of fight, and Hitler had already demonstrated his aversion to any kind of defensive operations.

However, intelligence reports had been erring on the side of giving credence to these rumors. So, although Patton was not of the opinion that much resistance would be found in the Alps (in his snarky recollection, "it was obvious to me that the end of the war was very close"), Third Army was redirected southwards into Austria in a sweeping right-turn. [18, 19]

The movement did not entirely keep Patton out of Czechoslovakia, even though it had technically been assigned to the sphere of the ever-approaching Red Army. As Third Army made their last oblique maneuver of the war, accompanied by the Seventh Army to their south, they claimed the capture of Pilzen and Linz. Virtually no resistance was offered. German troops either continued to surrender en masse, melted into the picturesque Alpine villages, or simply died futilely, in small groups. There was no fortress, no last stand to be had high above the clouds, no Wagnerian final act.

On April 30, Hitler shot himself in his bunker in Berlin with Russian forces closing in. A week later, the remnants of the German military formally surrendered. There would be no need to advance farther.

May-June

The last month of the war had seen the 411th shuttled rapidly around Germany. The average American would not recognize the flurry of village names that appeared on the unit's location report: Eisenach on April 9; Tonndorf on the 14th; Ilmenau, Lohr, and Hohenchambach thereafter. The battalion was in a place named Wallersdorf, northeast of Munich, when the cease-fire was signed. There, at 5:36 AM on May 9, it received the official word that its role of providing anti-aircraft protection had finished. The unit remained in Wallersdorf until May 22, one day after the three-year anniversary of its inception. [1,2]

The end of formal fighting did not, of course, mean that an imminent departure of the Great Crusade was in order. Apart from the tremendous logistical problem of simply shipping back such an enormous host of soldiers and equipment, there were still towns to rebuild, roads to repair, partisans to track down, and treasure caches to guard.

In this interim period, a detachment of the 411th had made their way south into the vicinity of Salzburg and the infamous region of Berchtesgaden. Here, high in the snow-capped peaks, lay Hitler's famous *Kehlsteinhaus* – the Eagle's Nest, named for the *Kehlstein* peak on which it sat. Sited near the more famous *Berghof*, which was commonly used as a residence for the Fuhrer during the war, the less-frequented Eagle's Nest offered a view that could only overwhelm Hitler's visitors. Its construction at the edge of an almost inaccessible peak gave it a unique vantage point over the heart of the Nazi realms. From here, the devil could show his guests all the kingdoms of the world.

The exact identity of the unit that first captured the promontory is still up for debate, but the 101st Airborne's claim for this feat is probably the most famous. At any rate, by the end of the war, the site had become something of a tourist attraction for American GI's. The detachment from the 411th was on such a mission of military tourism. My grandfather was with them.

In the photos that survived of this trip, my grandfather is accompanied by two of the men who served as his jeep drivers. Their group had climbed around to the front face of the Eagle's Nest, giving a viewpoint opposite that which typically adorns modern postcard images. There, they can be seen sitting on a hillside, Bavaria at their feet, behind the photographer.

I find this particular scene to be terribly poetic. If World War II was a hurricane, then the Kehlsteinhaus sat right in its metaphorical eye. It lay near the center of what was once Fortress Europe, *Festung Europa*, as the world swirled into chaos around it. But, it was ultimately a house, a home even, replete with dining and sitting areas: all things considered, a pleasant indoor environment.

Through the intervention of megalomania and evil, however, an object that normally would be little more than a

The Kehlsteinhaus - Perched in the Eagle's Nest

footnote in civil engineering lore was transformed in the minds of the public into a symbol of the Nazi regime. There is nothing particularly sinister about the place. There were no mass murders committed here, no enormous armored actions carried out, no frenzied party rallies or world-changing assassinations brought to fruition. Yet, the mountain became an invaluable stop for those who were on a pilgrimage to tour the lives of those who had caused the world so much pain. It had taken on a life of its own, imbued with an ethos and a mythology absorbed from the men who had ventured onto it a comparative handful of times.

The house at the top of the the Kehlstein, then, is a vessel. It carries the fleeting memories of historic evil in what is, ultimately, a quirk of construction: it is, simply, built very high in the clouds. Like spilled paint seeping into the cracks of a very coarse layer of brick, the house's aura was kept alive in the public's mind by its idiosyncrasy of elevation, which also probably spared it from demolition, the fate of the far more significant (but less fantastical) *Berghof*.

View from an Alpine Height

    The conclusion that memories can be selectively imprinted on a place by society is certainly not a shocking one. But, it does raise one point worthy of reflection. We have seen that idiosyncrasy, when touched by evil, remains associated with evil. What happens when idiosyncrasy is touched by happiness and joy? Is there something buried deep within human feeling that makes the preservation of evil easier? Or, is the retention of love just as straightforward? To answer a question like this, it is difficult to look at the level of the historical record. A better example could perhaps be found by examining the personal sphere. As homes with quirks go, a better example than my grandparents' would be difficult to find.

    Notwithstanding their few-but-impactful wartime years, my grandparents lived most of their lives in a single-story, red-brick house in the town of Liberty Boro, a neighboring community of McKeesport, Pennsylvania. Liberty was highly intertwined with McKeesport, to the point that my their mailing address actually listed the latter as their place of residence. Both were towns that, earlier in the century, surged with the power of American industry. Sited on the southern bank of the Youghiogheny River, downstream from the renowned Edgar Thomson steel works made famous by Andrew Carnegie, McKeesport boasted impressive metal processing firepower in its own right.

The town sprung up around this heavy industry during the early part of the 20th century, peaking at well over 50,000 during the postwar years. It was then that my grandparents first moved into their abode on 'C' street, perhaps a a couple tenths of a mile from the Youghiogheny, just southwest of 'B' and 'A' streets. Alphabetical exactitude apparently trumped descriptive power in the town planners' minds.

By the time the 1950's ended and the steel industry began to decline, the population of the area steadily eroded. Few new housing developments were built, and, forty years later, much of Liberty Boro seemed frozen in time. Block after block of amply-spaced brick houses remained unchanged, inhabited by an aging population: a monument to the home lives of the Greatest Generation.

My grandparents' house was no exception; the frequent visits there that I experienced as a child constantly impressed upon me how close the events of several decades past could actually remain. The house was a welcoming museum, a mirror that peered back five decades.

    I remember so many trivial things about it: the front door opening directly into the living room, with no foyer in between; a Wolmanized wood fence that wrapped around the back yard in a terribly confusing polygon; the concrete shower that was placed haphazardly, randomly, in the basement.

    I remember that back yard and the many iterations it experienced over the years. In it, my grandfather always maintained a tidy garden guarded by his red wooden fence. Although at one point the garden actually boasted a full-grown apple tree, its trademark was the plump, juicy tomatoes that he would harvest en masse year after year. His secret? Sowing sugar with the tomatoes so that the roots would grow while drinking the botanical equivalent of soda pop. Outlandish, yes, but we certainly never argued with the results of such innovation.

    Just before reaching the back yard, on the house's eastern face, a side entrance that led into the kitchen was sited. The kitchen itself was decked out in all the glory of the late 1950's: orangeish tile, a quarter-circular breakfast nook with faded cushions, and a noticeable lack of an electric dishwasher.

    Beyond those traits, though, was the comically-small stove that my grandmother would use to cook meals when the family would congregate. Somehow, this undersized little box would pump out mashed potatoes and pasta at a preternaturally rapid pace. Thanksgiving dinners and casual lunches would fly out of the worn sauce pots that adorned the stovetop onto aging dishes. I never remember the food being anything other than delectable.

    An entrance to the basement was located in one corner of the kitchen. There, my grandfather had built a darkroom. After returning from WWII, he had elected to depart from industrial work and had chosen to pursue a career in photography. He obtained a job at Bettis Laboratories, a nearby government nuclear facility, where he worked until his retirement a few decades later. From that point forward, his photographic work was done on an exclusively freelance basis, and his darkroom served as his center of operations.

    As the world shifted to one of hand-held Nikon film cameras and 24-hour drugstore photo development, and as my grandfather began to age, the darkroom eventually lost its utility. It was transitioned into a storage complex that housed boxes of random paraphernalia, piled high to the ceiling. After my grandparents had departed the house, my parents and I spent days sifting through the relics of that room. Of particular interest were turn-of-the-century Kodak camera parts and development technology, stamped "Made In America," a distinguishing fact of its own merit.

    I remember so much else of that place, but the most important part was that it housed my grandparents. When I visited them, I was visiting a grandfather who had seen the worst war in history, who had actually played a role, however minor, on the biggest stage imaginable, and who, fifty years later, was able to sit down with me, smile, and love in a way that was fully divorced from the terrors of armed combat.

If Hitler and the Nazi party had left their imprint on a place that rested at history's center-of-mass by merely skirting its location on several occasions, my grandfather could claim to have left his signature on a site that rested at history's fringe after having imbued it with his presence for so many years. Memory is not confined to a particular class of historical being. Although history itself is a record of that which is remembered, it is also a reflection on the willingness of the descendants of history's characters *to* remember. As such, both the brick house on C Street and the Eagle's Nest belong to the same class of dwellings: places imprinted with either the good or the evil of human nature in a way that associates them with their owners, regardless of the broader flow of history.

****

The 411th would eventually be shipped home to Hampton Roads in October, 1945, well after VJ day and the final ending of the war. Prior to that happy event, however, there was one grisly last stop for the battalion. On June 27, the unit rolled into Munich for a month's-long stint on garrison duty. What they found there had already sickened thousands who had passed through the city before them.

The first of the Nazi concentration camps were uncovered way back in early April in the vicinity of XII Corps, outside of Ohrdruf and Weimar. Patton and his staff were so disgusted with what they found that they insisted on forcing the German inhabitants of the nearby areas to go through the camps to look upon their government's handiwork. Famously, the mayor of one of these towns committed suicide with his wife after doing so. After Eisenhower was called in to view the scene, he inquired of an infantryman who happened to be close by, 'Still having trouble hating them?' [3]

The ensuing weeks saw more camps liberated by advancing Allied troops, everywhere provoking nausea, fury, and bewilderment. The ghastly incinerators of human bodies, scaffolds, and darkened torture chambers provoked those two inevitable questions: 'What kind of people are these that we are fighting?' and 'What kind of people are *we*?' Even for troops who had been in the thick of the worst kind of combat, the tramp of thousands of human skeletons and the sight of decayed corpses piled like firewood was an unsettling sight of the most terrible sort.

Probably the worst discovery, however, at least on the western side of Europe, came on April 29, when the camp outside of Munich was overrun. As Rod Serling would speak of it a decade later, this camp in particular was "a monument to a moment in time when some men decided to turn the Earth into a graveyard. Into it they shoveled all of their reason, their logic, their knowledge, but worst of all, their conscience." The place, of course, was Dachau, and it still kept some 31,000 individuals hostage as of the day of its liberation. [4]

Diving into a deep exploration of the nature of the Holocaust is not something that I am prepared to do. It is an area that touches on the worst possible aspects of the human mind while simultaneously sickening the stomach and raising that most incontrovertible question of 'Why?' To try to treat it with any form of thoroughness in a short space would not be just. Suffice it to say that the torments that existed on a magnitude afflicting one particular camp that housed tens-of-thousands could not be washed away in the span of just a few months. When the 411th rolled into Munich in late June, then, even though the main mass of bodies had been carted away, the area had hardly been fully sanitized.

My grandfather barely spoke of D Battery's time here. Apart from some comments about the terrible smell and the unnervingly large number of decomposing bodies that he had once made to my mother, he never bothered to describe his unit's experiences. The words of another member of the battalion who was there survived, though:

> You'd seen the newsreels and articles about this place. It's all just the way they've given it out to the public, the worst kind of hole in Germany. They were so cruel to the people here, so cruel and inhuman I can't help wanting to punish

these sons of [redacted] myself. How anyone could be that way is beyond me...

The fellows that took over the place from the Krauts were still here and have given us all we could stand to listen to. They saw the trains full of the dead... It's cleaned up a great deal now. ⁵

Ultimately, the view at Dachau, even after two months of cleaning, was a sight that man was not meant to see. The citizen-soldier who encountered that infamous *Arbeit Macht Frei* signage was out of his depth. He was treading in the maw of evil, tiptoing at the event horizon that marked the edge of a person's humanity. The distinguishing characteristic of most of these soldiers back in the States, a tranquil, non-violent life, simply had no meaning past those iron bars. The type of love that a man could show for his family, even after fighting on the battlefield, the grateful appreciation for a quiet life that could be found by those who survived the bullets of the Wehrmacht, was mocked by the lingering misery that lay in the camp. As I see it, for my grandfather and for others who found Dachau, or Auschwitz, or Buchenwald, or any of the other camps, to be their last stop in the European Theater, the lingering subconscious quandary that must have been present was the reconciling what they had seen with how they would live the rest of their lives.

The viewing of a concentration camp, then, is a most terrible thing; to have actually participated in its atrocities, an unavoidably and inherently bestial, murderous act. These statements argue that both the soldier-observer and the perpetrator must live a life of hatred: the one, for vengeance, the other, out of evil. The question of how a citizen-soldier responds to this, whether such a malign influence persists after his sword becomes a plowshare, therefore becomes a meditation on the nature of hate and its development. Can hate be released after viewing such an execrable sight? What should take its place? Is it a just thing to do no more than merely remember and educate? I am sure that the haunted look and sickened glance that crept upon my grandfather's features when he gave the briefest description of his time in Dachau to my mother was due in large part to an awareness of these questions.

The 411th left Dachau and Munich on July 21, 1945. Just over three months later, the unit arrived in Virginia. Their war was complete.

Epilogue

This is the extent of the chronicle that I can give of my grandfather's time in the Second World War. Like all history, the telling of it consists of conveying sometimes-jumbled anecdotes, official records, and broader connections to a wider world. The essence, though, as always, must lie with the individual man and his interactions both with others and with his own psyche.

I suppose that the question posed some twenty-odd-thousand words ago, on the nature of hatred and how it tied into the broader existence and mental state of the citizen-soldier still remains unanswered. The fury that must be felt on the front lines against an enemy seeking to deliver death, or within the confines of a reeking concentration camp, is obviously something that is difficult, if not impossible, to dissect. Similarly, the peaceful aspects of everyday life have an infinite variety of flavors.

With this theme in mind, then, a major underlying problem is that there are radically different types of hate and love. A child will report that he *hates* broccoli and *loves* ice cream. He will also tell you that he *hates* a particular teacher at school for giving too much homework and *loves* another for his easy policies. To what extent, then, does this hate and this love differ from a Nazified hatred of Jews or the love for a comrade found on the battlefield? Is it a question of extent? Can it be truly reasonable to presume that hatred of leafy vegetables and a desire for genocide are only separated by the extremity of the subject being detested? We can ask a similar question of the spectrum of love.

For the latter, Greek philosophy and Christian theology certainly answer in the negative. We can count at least three different classifications of love in classical teachings: *eros, philia,* and *agape*. Commonly stated, these are sexual love, brotherly love, and divine love. The three differ from each other not in their intensity, but in the humanly and spiritual dimension which they encompass. To speak in a simplified mathematical sense, they are orthogonal to each other. Their components need not intersect.

Without necessarily assuming that hate completes a duality with love, is it too large of a leap to conclude that there must be different, orthogonal, types of hatred? As a modern society, we tend to incorrectly conflate *eros* with its brothers. Perhaps the same could be said of our thoughts on the contrast between a venomous, haughty, despising sort of hate and a weary, resigned fury. To an outsider, they could certainly appear the same. The type of anger that would accompany both is the sort of thing that those unaccustomed to the fires of war would regard with terror.

Yet, I believe that the second type of hatred can ultimately be distinguished as a lamentation manifested in a *forward* form, in the style of the old motivational prose, "if you are going through hell, keep going." The hatred is not, in itself, directed towards the aim of destruction, even if its collateral impact is that of widespread devastation. Rather, it is the same hate that a wildcat trapped in a net feels: rage against the cords that are holding it in place, a desire to slash those entrapping binds to ribbons. The animal itself wants its predicament to *end*. It wants its life back. It hates, but not with a malevolent hatred.

Contrast this an arrogant despisement, a bloodthirsty desire for mayhem. An example of this would be found in the annals of Tamerlane, who was famous for building pyramids of hundreds of thousands of human skulls in the centers of slaughtered cities. This hatred is not *forward*. It is self-sustaining, and it exists for its own ends, be these the prideful conquest of lesser peoples on the Asian steppe or the scientific massacre of a race deemed to be intrinsically inferior.

The distinction between the two forms of hate is not sharply defined. Consider the following story. Drew Middleton, a correspondent for the New York Times in the Western Theater, found himself observing the urban fighting around Aachen in October of 1944. Embroiled in the bloody, house-to-house, block-by-block advance of the Big Red One, he could see the brutal point-blank artillery tactics that GI's used to blow away dug-in Nazi formations. Middleton also encountered a sight that he found sufficiently troubling to warrant a particular mention.

As part of the urban combat, it would have been common for ruined buildings to become miniature fortresses.

Middleton came across one of these small bastions, in the form of a bedroom that overlooked a nearby road. It was garrisoned by a solitary infantryman and draped in colored quilts, the trappings of devastated civility. The soldier had been pursuing a one-man vendetta in the midst of the larger war. Pumping relentless fire from his rifle into the street below, the GI was muttering darkly, 'The sons of bitching bastards. The fucking, fucking bastards.' [1] The profanity and the bullets rained down onto whatever Nazi interlopers happened to be nearby, hastening their demise and the taking of Aachen.

What can be made of this particular GI's case? Certainly, such vitriol against an enemy is nothing unique, whitewashed, nonmilitary images of heroism notwithstanding. But, is it even possible for an outside observer to conclude the nature of this man's hatred? Can we undoubtedly pass judgment on him as being nothing more than a less-powerful, non-Asiatic Tamerlane? The answer appears obvious: only the man himself can give an accurate depiction of his psyche's state. Like any emotional judgment, this is a question that only the individual can answer.

But, even to an outside observer, it is clear that Middleton's soldier is sitting precariously between definitions of hate. To be melodramatic, his soul is effectively hanging in the metaphorical balance, for it seems clear that the two types of hatred are not morally equivalent.

Equally clear, though, is that this man did not will the events that led to his miserable stint in Aachen into being. I would venture a guess that he was not a career soldier, that he was swept along with the tide of the Great Crusade like the vast majority of his comrades. He was thrown into an internal moral conflict by forces far beyond his control, and a decision was demanded of him: which side of his humanity would he support? Such a struggle is every bit as epic as an armored advance by Third Army's Shermans.

If, then, there is a struggle, there must be an opportunity for glory, as, however glory, or valor, or greatness, is defined, any combat offers its participants a scale-the-ramparts type of moment. In this case, glory comes from an act of the will. It derives from not passing from the second form of hatred into the first form. It comes from resisting the urge to throw aside whatever trappings of peaceful life would prevent a wholesale descent into a love of slaughter. It is the exercising of the human ability to declare, *this far, and no farther*.

It continues towards the form of recognizing what must come after the danger is over, the guns are silent, and the enemy is vanquished. Such glory would not end with the cessation of battle; rather, it is then that it finds its true form in the transition to a time of peace.

Perhaps I am biased in this view by the fact that this is the path my grandfather took. Certainly, of the millions of men that were sent into battle in the Second World War, there were countless outcomes that show that Sherman's bitter axiom of 'War is Hell' still applies in its most unvarnished form. Those outcomes truly let us think of battle as a deep, dark abyss which sucks all that is good in the world into a vortex of smoke, cinders, and thunder. There is no glory in these outcomes. There is only fury and despair. Distinguishing between two forms of hatred is a fruitless and empty endeavor in these cases, because there is no *forward* movement.

Ultimately, as a noncombatant, I am hamstrung in advancing a counterpoint, that there may, in fact, be glory after all, glory that might end in love and a triumph over darker forces. The experiences that I have of war are little better than voyeuristic. Consumption of the memories of men *who were there* is a tonic for the mind in that it opens up the possibility of an existence unfathomable to those who have not tasted battle. That, however, is as much as it can do. I can no more offer a true exploration of the philosophy of the battlefield than I can give a firsthand description of the stench of seared flesh in the Norman countryside or of the thud of rifle bullets knifing through frozen human bodies in the Ardennes. I, like all noncombatants who simply want to understand the mind of the soldier, am saddled with a reluctantly grateful ignorance about these matters.

But, even if this type of knowledge is beyond my grasp, does that necessarily mean that I cannot evince some natural comprehension of the citizen-soldier's psyche based purely on an attempt to reconcile the civilian postwar life with the known horrors of war, however lacking an understanding of the latter is?

If the answer to the question above is 'no,' then I submit the following, as a humble statement on a topic about which I do not have the life experience to declare true understanding: my grandfather, like so many of his cohorts, was a hero. He won glory, not 'on the line,' but in his noble deportment in the middle of the action and in the face of evil. His triumph lay in the very nature of his journey from civilian life, to the battlefield, and back to a new family. In the process, he never found his soul so sullied by death and fury that it could not find its way home.

****

My grandfather died on July 23, 2007. I had seen him last a few short days prior, and, although his voice had failed him and his once tall, muscular form was now unable to leave his bed in the assisted-living home, the love in his eyes when he spied me was undiminished. I would like to think that his final thoughts were of the love returned by his family, by his God, and by me.

The pre-funeral viewing was held shortly thereafter. Of that day, I remember two specific things.

The first was the book that I was reading in our car's backseat during the long, rainy drive to the funeral parlor in

Liberty Boro. It was a piece on military history by Max Boot, titled *War Made New*. It explored how militaries evolved over the centuries via particular revolutions in thinking and technology.

One idea that Boot emphasized early in the book was:

> ...that countries able to take advantage of these shifts have been history's winners while those that have fallen behind in harnessing military innovations have usually been consigned to irrelevance or oblivion [2]

My young mind grasped upon this as an argument that history was shaped by military events first and foremost. Wars and armies, then, were the true movers of history. Thus, the soldier, as the key cog to those wars and armies, was, in turn, the true mover behind them. Perhaps this is not what Mr. Boot intended to convey, but it was a message that stuck nonetheless.

The second memorable event was what occurred at sunset.

By the evening, all of the attendees apart from my parents and I had filtered out. I was finally left alone as the two of them meandered over to our parked car. I had my last unspoken conversation with my grandfather at that moment.

Throughout the day, exposed to the awful task of socializing with a muted sea of black-garbed relatives, I had let my mind wander to the injustice of the fact that though my grandfather had certainly been labelled a *good* man, he would never be regarded as a *great* man. He would boast no marble busts, no poetry, no cultural awareness. His life would not be recorded by a modern-day Plutarch if a *Lives of the Noble Americans* ever were to exist.

But then my mind began to wander to the ways in which he was a superlative in every possible way.

He had been a representative of the Greatest Generation, an unnamed member of the Allied Expeditionary Force's Great Crusade. He was a part of a larger self as surely as any legionary was who fought beside Caesar at Alesia, or with Napoleon at Borodino. He was an actor on a world stage. He had a bit part, true, but it was the part of a citizen-soldier, that most gallant of professions. He found his way home when the fighting ceased and made that most wrenching transition from warrior to civilian. He beat his sword into a plowshare, took up a happy and productive profession, and started a family. He loved, and lived the rest of his life in peace.

As I left the funeral parlor that night, I couldn't help tearfully murmuring to myself, aware of the grandiosity of my words, "Rest in peace, Great Man."

For Pappy

Bibliography

411th AAR's, Kill Accounts, and Location Records, [AAR, KA, LR]. Copies made from War Department documents in National Archives, St. Louis. 1942-1945.
411th Commendations. Haislip, Fraser, et al. US Army war records, declassified. 1944.
Ambrose, Steven E. *The Wild Blue,* [TWB]. Simon & Schuster, NY, 2001.
Ambrose, Steven E. *Citizen Soldiers*, [CS]. Simon & Schuster, NY, 1997.
Atkinson, Rick. *An Army at Dawn,* [AAD] Henry Holt & Co., NY, 2002.
Atkinson, Rick. *The Guns at Last Light*, [TGLL]. Henry Holt & Co., NY, 2013.
Boot, Max. *War Made New: Weapons, Warriors, and the Making of the Modern World*. Gotham Books, NY, 2006.
Ebert, Roger. Review of *Saving Private Ryan.*
http://www.rogerebert.com/reviews/saving-private-ryan-1998. 1998.
Gavin, James M. *On To Berlin*. Viking, NY, 1978.
Livius, Titus Quinctius. *The Early History of Rome*. Tr. Aubrey de Sèlincourt. Penguin, London, 1960.
Manchester, William, and Paul Reid. *The Last Lion: Defender of the Realm.* Little, Brown & Co., NY, 2012.
O'Brien, Tim in *On War: The Best Military Histories*. Pritzker Military Museum & Library, Chicago, 2013. From *The Things They Carried*, Houghton Mifflin, 1990.
Patton, George S. *War As I Knew It*. Houghton Mifflin, NY, 1947.
Pyle, Ernie. *Here Is Your War*. Henry Holt & Co., NY, 1943.
Rogers, Norma. *Until the Final Gun*. 2002.
Serling, Rod. Quote from *Death's-Head Revisited*. From IMDB:
http://www.imdb.com/title/tt0734563/trivia?tab=qt&ref_=tt_trv_qu.
Sulzberger, C.L. *American Heritage Picture History of World War II*. Bonanza, NY, 1966.
Tyndall, Clifford. Greetings From Camp *Davis*. 2006.
OOB, June 6. http://www.6juin1944.com/assaut/utah/page.php?page=fo1_11. Accessed 07/2015.

Notes

Introduction
(1)   AAD, 9
(2)   Pyle, 195
(3, 4)   Boot, 59
(5)   Livius, 1

June-July
(1)   Sulzberger, 496
(2)   TGLL, 38
(3)   Manchester, 840
(4)   TGLL, 48-50
(5)   Gavin, 111
(6)   D-Day OOB
(7)   TGLL, 61
(8)   TWB, 23, 126
(9)   TGLL, 80
(10) Tyndall, 2, 107, 109, 195
(11) Rogers, 152, 195
(12) TGLL, 111
(13) TGLL, 139
(14) TGLL, 145
(15) Ebert
(16) O'Brien, 232

August
(1)   TGLL, 149
(2)   TGLL, 168
(3)   Rogers, 277
(4)   CS, 98
(5)   TGLL, 177
(6)   Manchester, 868
(7)   Rogers, 277
(8)   AAR, Unit commendations from Haislip/Fraser

(9) Patton, xii

September-November
(1) TGLL, 220-222
(2) CS, 119-131
(3) AAR: September
(4) Rogers, 300
(5) TGLL, 337-349
(6) CS, 136
(7) CS, 136-140; Patton, 146-147
(8) TGLL, 291-326
(9) CS, 260
(10) TGLL, 339-340
(11) TGLL, 344-349; Patton, 177
(12) CS, 158-162 (State of replacements); TGLL 408
(13) Patton, 172-173
(14) TGLL, 250

December
(1) Patton, 184-186
(2) CS, 266
(3) Rogers, 353
(4) Pyle, *13*
(5) TGLL, 421-438
(6) CS, 205
(7) TGLL, 460
(8) CS, 224-225
(9) TGLL, 450-467
(10) KA: December
(11) Patton, 202

January-April

(1) Patton, 209-210
(2) TGLL, 482-486
(3) AAR: January
(4) KA; LR: Early 1945
(5) CS, 395-400
(6) TGLL, 524-541
(7) Patton, 251-252
(8) Patton, 230
(9) TGLL, 546-555
(10) Patton, 273-
(11) Manchester, 907
(12) TGLL, 560
(13) Rogers, 409
(14) Rogers, 417
(15) CS, 445-449
(16) Patton, 283-287
(17) TGLL, 595
(18) CS, 456-457
(19) Patton, 309

May-June

(1) LR: May, June
(2) Rogers, 442
(3) TGLL, 590-614
(4) Serling
(5) Rogers, 464

Epilogue

(1) TGLL, 294
(2) Boot, 16

Made in the USA
Middletown, DE
22 April 2016